Looking for Your Name

A RICHARD JACKSON BOOK

Also by Paul B. Janeczko

POETRY COLLECTIONS

Strings: *A Gathering of Family Poems*

Pocket Poems

Poetspeak: *In Their Work, About Their Work*

Dont Forget to Fly

Postcard Poems

Going Over to Your Place: *Poems for Each Other*

This Delicious Day: *65 Poems*

The Music of What Happens: *Poems That Tell Stories*

The Place My Words Are Looking For

Preposterous: *Poems of Youth*

ORIGINAL POETRY

Brickyard Summer

FICTION

Bridges to Cross

NONFICTION

Loads of Codes and Secret Ciphers

Looking for Your Name

A COLLECTION OF CONTEMPORARY POEMS

Selected by Paul B. Janeczko

ORCHARD BOOKS NEW YORK

Orchard Books, 95 Madison Avenue, New York, NY 10016

Manufactured in the United States of America
Book design by Mina Greenstein
The text of this book is set in 11 point Times Roman.
10 9 8 7 6 5 4 3 2 1

Library of Congress Cataloging-in-Publication Data
Looking for your name : a collection of contemporary poems /
selected by Paul B. Janeczko. p.   cm. Includes index.
Summary: Poems which present a wide-ranging look at life in
contemporary America.
ISBN 0-531-05475-6.   ISBN 0-531-08625-9 (lib. bdg.)
1. Young adult poetry, American. 2. American poetry—
20th century. [1. American poetry.] I. Janeczko, Paul B.
PS586.3L66 1993 811'.540809283–dc20 92-25648

for John Janeczko,

brother and sidekick,
through crewcuts
Callicoon
the Kingston Trio
collisions in short left field
and wagon wrecks on 14th Street

Contents

Raising My Hand, *Antler*   *1*

1

In the lonely games no one sees the wonderful things you do

I Have Some Questions about Life on Earth,
   Del Marie Rogers   *5*
Stripped, *George Ella Lyon*   *7*
The Nuclear Accident at SL 1, Idaho Falls, 1961,
   Judith Vollmer   *8*
White Trash, *Jim Hall*   *9*
For Generations, *Charles Harper Webb*   *10*

Modern Times, *James Nolan*   *12*
Restoring the Ecology, *Leo Dangel*   *13*
The Black Thumb, *Ronald Koertge*   *14*
Letting the Plants Die, *Myra Sklarew*   *15*
Morning Glory, *Howard Nemerov*   *16*
Purple Loosestrife, *Ann Townsend*   *17*

Distance, *Jim Simmerman*   *18*
Lonely Games, *David Evans, Jr.*   *19*
Play, *Ann Townsend*   *20*
Why I Quit Dancing Lessons, *Gary Gildner*   *21*
Live Studio Wrestling, *Jim Hall*   *22*
Wrestling to Lose, *Geof Hewitt*   *23*
Ice Hockey, *Jonathan Holden*   *24*

Coach Goes down the Hall Wondering Where All
   the Men Went, *Jack Ridl*   *25*
Karate, *Jonathan Holden*   *26*
The Rodeo Fool, *Walter McDonald*   *27*
Challenge, *Samuel Hazo*   *29*
Tom Lonehill (1940–1956), *David Allan Evans*   *30*

I Hear the River Call My Name, *Sheryl L. Nelms*   *32*
The Suicide's Father, *Baron Wormser*   *33*
Pulling Peter Back, *Christine Hemp*   *34*
No Woman Is Ever Prepared, *Deborah Bosley*   *35*
Thinking about Bill, Dead of AIDS, *Miller Williams*   *36*
The Enticing Lane, *Christopher Hewitt*   *37*
Identifying Things, *Wendy Barker*   *39*
For Poppa, Asleep in the Smithtown Madhouse,
   Peter Serchuk   *41*

The Old Man & His Calf, *Keith Wilson*   *43*
Old Red, *Kathleen Iddings*   *43*
i'll never, *Todd Moore*   *45*
Leaving, *Judith W. Steinbergh*   *46*
How to Take a Walk, *Leo Dangel*   *46*
Burying, *Paul Ruffin*   *47*
Killing the Dog, *Robert Morgan*   *48*
Confession, Curse and Prayer, *Paul Zimmer*   *49*
Ineffable Beauty, *James Strecker*   *50*

Waiting for the Splash, *Ralph Fletcher*   *52*
To an Estranged Wife, *Gary Young*   *52*
Even When, *Christine Hemp*   *53*
He Attempts to Love His Neighbors, *Alden Nowlan*   *53*
When Leland Left Elma, *Ree Young*   *55*

The View, *Philip Schultz*   56
Talking Long Distance after One A.M., *Mary Clark*   57
The Two Orders of Love, *Edward Field*   58
Gone Astray: Little Miss Muffet, *David James*   59
Help Is on the Way, *Herbert Scott*   60
The Visiting Paleontologist Feels Her Thigh,
   Grace Bauer   62
After Quarreling, *R. T. Smith*   63
married 3 months, *Sheryl L. Nelms*   65
The Belt Buckle, *Leo Dangel*   65
Newlyweds, *David Evans, Jr.*   66
Anna Marie, *Peter Oresick*   68
Gossip, *Judith W. Steinbergh*   69
Appearances, *Phil Hey*   69

2

America,
it's hard to get your attention

Patriotics, *David Baker*   73
When Bosses Sank Steel Islands, *Alice Fulton*   74
Out of the Mines, *Gary Young*   75
Blue Collar, *John M. Roderick*   76
No Job, *Jim Daniels*   77
The Market Economy, *Marge Piercy*   79

Bones in an African Cave, *Peter Meinke*   81
House Keys, *Vic Coccimiglio*   82
wounds #13, *Safiya Henderson-Holmes*   82
The Burnt Child, *Herbert Scott*   83
Flames, *Ronald Wallace*   83
Harold Iverson, Teacher, *Rodney Torreson*   84
Sister, *Kathleen Iddings*   86
Recurrence, *Jane Wilson Joyce*   86
What Holds Us Back, *Liz Rosenberg*   87

The Best Dance Hall in Iuka, Mississippi, *Thomas Johnson* 88
The Failures of Pacifism, *Ronald Wallace* 88
Why I'm in Favor of a Nuclear Freeze,
    Christopher Buckley 89

Why Is It, *Robert A. Fink* 91
Shipping Out, *Joan LaBombard* 92
Conscientious Objector, *Henry Carlile* 93
Matthew Schnell, *Rodney Torreson* 93
Hunting on the Homefront, *Bill Dodd* 95
War, *Katherine Soniat* 96
Airplane Conversation with an Engineer Who Designed
    Ammunition, *Mary Ann Waters* 97
The Food Pickers of Saigon, *Walter McDonald* 98
The Penance, *Leonard Nathan* 100
Vietnam War Memorial, *Robert Morgan* 101
Saying Farewell, He Shows Me His Vietnam Poems,
    Ray Gonzalez 102
The Challenge, *Geof Hewitt* 103
the hard way, *Sheryl L. Nelms* 103
In San Salvador (I), *Grace Paley* 104
Aftermath, *June Jordan* 105
Poem Ending with an Old Cliché, *Paul Zimmer* 105

Family Portrait 1933, *Peter Oresick* 107
Family, *Grace Paley* 108
Four Roses, *Susan Wood* 108
The Most Haunted, *Robert Louthan* 109
For a Sister Not Yet Dead, *Elliot Fried* 110
anorexia neurosis, *Sheryl L. Nelms* 111
Winter Stars, *Larry Levis* 112
The Absent Father, *Lee Sharkey* 114
Jack's Flashlight, *Chase Twichell* 115

My Mother, If She Had Won Free Dance Lessons,
  Cornelius Eady   *116*
Nursing Home, *Sam Cornish*   *117*
Moving My Grandfather, *Jim Daniels*   *118*
Eastern Standard, *David Huddle*   *119*
His Grandmother Talks about God, *Paul Ruffin*   *120*
Heaven for Railroad Men, *David Wojahn*   *121*
To My Sons on Father's Day, *Robert A. Fink*   *123*
Eye of the Beholder, *Mark Vinz*   *124*
Tristem, *Dorianne Laux*   *125*
Family, *Del Marie Rogers*   *126*

Delicate, *Matthew Graham*   *127*

Acknowledgments   *128*
Index of First Lines   *136*
Index of Authors and Titles   *139*

Looking for Your Name

Raising My Hand

ANTLER

One of the first things we learn in school is
    if we know the answer to a question
We must raise our hand and be called on
    before we can speak.
How strange it seemed to me then,
    raising my hand to be called on,
How at first I just blurted out,
    but that was not permitted.

How often I knew the answer
And the teacher (knowing I knew)
Called on others I knew (and she knew)
    had it wrong!
How I'd stretch my arm
    as if it would break free
    and shoot through the roof
    like a rocket!
How I'd wave and groan and sigh,
Even hold up my aching arm
    with my other hand
Begging to be called on,
Please, *me*, I know the answer!
Almost leaping from my seat
    hoping to hear my name.

Twenty-nine now, alone in the wilds,
Seated on some rocky outcrop
    under all the stars,
I find myself raising my hand
    as I did in first grade
Mimicking the excitement
    and expectancy felt then.
No one calls on me
    but the wind.

1

In the lonely games
no one sees
the wonderful things
you do

I Have Some Questions about Life on Earth

DEL MARIE ROGERS

Why did the trees stop casting
the benevolent shadow we felt in childhood?
The furniture of the dead is scattered
in all directions, wind polishes it,
it will never belong indoors again,
it will be part of the soil, or stay
in someone else's house
like a stone brought in from the fields.
Why do houses that were filled with love
stand empty?

The plum tree's in full bloom,
a petal floats on the lake
and a little boy has been discovered
in his backyard swimming pool.
He was missing for months, found
when the ice melted, his cap floated
to the top of the water. His mother
looked for days in the snow,
he was missing at Christmas.

People are born without shelter
in the streets of Teheran,
they live in holes underground.
A friend took me to see the house
of the young Shah in Lubbock—
it looked like any other rich person's house,
many of them in that neighborhood.

Why is that young man, strong and black,
trapped in a cavern of walls, dead in advance,
pinned like a leaf to the wall of the future?

A girl stands before me,
healed cuts on her arms
because her mother, drunk, cold,
grabbed a butcher knife,
couldn't say anything strong enough
to show what held her.
In another city, black teenagers
poured gasoline over a white social worker
walking toward her stranded car,
set fire to her with their lighters.
Flaming, she walked the streets for help
but didn't find it in time.

Life is sweet, honeysuckle trails into the water
far back in the woods where no one sees it.
We eat plums, listen to meadowlarks
though we are walking in fire like these others.
The petals of our wars are falling,
each one marked with a death:
when I see the flowers in air
it scorches my soul like napalm,
clings to my body.
Our lives spiral out in our minds
like the movie's last reel, the end-piece flapping.

Cars stream over the hill,
migrating birds edge over the traffic
in a field of cloud. We are set down to live,
we stand tall and dark as we can
as the sky pours over us.
Sticky white and green wildflowers, star-shapes,
lie gentle, exposed under the clouds
on this gray day. Surprising
how wide-open the world is, available,
as if earth,

scraped, blasted, firebombed
remembers, listens,
and still has quietness
and still can be wounded.

Stripped

G E O R G E   E L L A   L Y O N

I was humming "Mist on the Mountain"
and shelling peas
I was figuring board feet
I was carting off stones
and quilting lettuce
and thinking about a baby
growing ripe inside
I was voting
I was lifting pain
out by the roots,
the bread indoors
breathing beneath a thin towel,
when a D-10 dozer came
and rolled me off the front porch.

The Nuclear Accident at SL 1, Idaho Falls, 1961

JUDITH VOLLMER

My father remembers a nurse
talking from her hospital bed,
off-limits in her dome, like a ghost
or captured angel, still full of what
she'd managed to do: climb the ladder,
free the man so hot they had to wait
before burying him, till they scraped
his skin and cleaned his bones.
After three weeks she was still alive
and slowly dying, telling the
ridiculous bad luck of it:

A guy's standing, settling the fuel bundle
into the reactor
and his buddy comes up and gooses him.
The bundle jerks, the lid of the great
vessel slides open and off. The guy
is blasted up
impaled to the ceiling
by a shaft of steam & a metal rod
his white-suited body
stuck up there
and no one,
all of them evacuated,
can get him down till
days later the medical team
enters the containment
in jumpsuits & booties.
My father remembers the nurse
entering the dome, pretty & bright.
It takes brilliance to be a heroine
& something secret & stupid.

She walks across the shining floor.
She places her foot on the first rung
then the next, climbs up.
She must know how stupid this is.
It's only a body up there
and the air is invisible
with what will kill her.
Has anyone given her anything to take along
on this trip? Rabbit foot? Heart on a chain?
Can she see anything in the face looking
down at her? She holds herself
up. She pulls him down.
She walks to the ambulance & lead coffin.
She knows what she is doing.
She knows what she has to do.

White Trash

J I M   H A L L

Now it's Styrofoam pellets
that blow across the yard.
They settle in the new grass
like the eggs of Japanese toys.
It's a kind of modern snowing.

The boy next door opened a box,
took out the precious present
and shook these white spun plastic
droplets into the wind.
It's how his family thinks.

Hundreds of them. Shaped like
unlucky fetuses or the brains
of TV stars.

Now they burrow in the lawn,
defy the rake, wriggle like the toes
of the shallow buried.

They'll be there when we're gone.
Bright tumors, rooted in the dark.
Crowding the dirt. Nothing makes them
grow. But nothing kills them either.

For Generations

C H A R L E S   H A R P E R   W E B B

Two Indians draped in buffalo robes
trudge across a crowded city park.
They wear pelts under their robes:
fox, rabbit, beaver, bear,
so many pelts the Indians could be

hairballs perched on toothpick legs.
They trudge because they wear snowshoes;
though there is no snow.
The sun glares, hot and bright.
Spring flowers sparkle everywhere.

"Where do you two think *you're* going!?"
a buffalo-faced policeman demands.
"We track the wandering herds,"
the lead Indian replies,
"as we have for generations."

Buffalo-face mumbles, "Oh."
The crowd parts like a white sea.
The Indians trudge through us,
heads down, leaning far forward
into what must be a bitter wind.

Modern Times

JAMES NOLAN

I have never signed
the peace pact with machinery
never can open car doors
or even a can for that matter.

I peck my way through typewriters
smudging and swearing like a coal miner
and always wind up with tape recorders
like an Englishman eating spaghetti.

The Indians signed it
and see what happened to them
herded by tractors onto reservations;
the immigrants signed it

and were stuffed into canneries
to baby-sit conveyor belts.
The President has signed it
even the Pope has signed it

but I will never sign
the peace pact with machinery
I will fight it tooth and throttle.
Every car that turns up my drive

is always carried off on a stretcher.
My record players become deaf mutes
my glare makes TVs catatonic and
vacuum cleaners bite the dust.

I live in a quiet rain forest
with no car and much license
where even the egg beater
is not my best friend.

Restoring the Ecology

LEO DANGEL

She has flowers
and plants I couldn't even name.
The colors can be pretty
when they bloom—yellow,
red, orange, blue, purple.
But mostly the house
is overgrown with green:
pots full of slough grass,
some plants with waxy leaves,
trees with giant fan leaves
like elephant ears.
I complained that I needed
a machete, that any day
we'd hear the shrill caw
of some jungle bird.

One day I put a few drops
of herbicide
into the old coffee pot
she uses to water the plants.
I didn't really want to kill
them all, only to thin things out.
But the herbicide finished off
everything except a cactus,
which she didn't water.
The house had the desolate look
of a destroyed rain forest.
"Why," she kept saying,
"did they all die like that?"

She was astonished
when I came home from town,
the pickup loaded down
with plants, and her delight
was something to see—
more plants than ever, some
she had never grown before.

Sometimes in the evening
when I sit reading my paper
and she's crocheting,
I look into the green around us
and imagine that a bird of paradise
is nesting somewhere back in there.

The Black Thumb

RONALD KOERTGE

He lived alone. Had a kitten but it died.
Got a puppy from the pound but it ran off
yelping.

One day he made a little garden out in back
of his rooming house and planted a few seeds.
They never came up.

A little later he bought a potted plant and
put it on top of the t.v. The next morning
even the dirt was gone.

On Saturday he went out to the park, lay
on his back and thought things over. When
he got up all the grass was yellow where
he'd been lying like a rock or something
had been there for months.

And you know that big tree out in Calif.
that's so famous and the cars can drive
through and all?

Well, that whole area is roped off and
troops are all over the place with orders
to shoot to kill.

Letting the Plants Die

MYRA   SKLAREW

This one's gone to straw   I cannot say
I'm sorry   and this one on the piano
is getting darker and stiff   I hardly look

but they leave their telltale signs
everywhere   the dry crisp leaves
on the window sill   the tendrils
hardened around the pillows of the sofa
the aphids vanished into the woodwork

The avocado is on its side   the Swedish
ivy I started from a cutting   the asparagus
fern spreading up the wall   daring to bloom
in winter

I am letting them die   glad to be free
of mist sprays and fertilizers   fish
emulsion I keep meaning to buy
free of double wavy blossoms   all
they ever had to offer

I hardly think of them anymore
walking through these rooms   but
sometimes I remember a man in a Greek
novel I was once reading   hovering
utterly naked behind his enormous
overgrown philodendron

The other side of the coin

Morning Glory

H O W A R D   N E M E R O V

Convolvulus it's called as well, or ill,
And bindweed, though sweating gardeners
Believe it rightly christened The Devil's Guts.

After it's tied whole hedges up in knots
And strangled all the flowers in a bed
And started to ambition after trees,

It opens out its own pale trumpet-belled
Five-bladed blooms—from white of innocence
Shading to heavenly blue—so frail they fall
At almost a touch, and even left alone
      Endure but a day.

Purple Loosestrife

A N N   T O W N S E N D

was too good to be true, in all its definitions.
Once beloved, once beautiful: today the wildflower magazines
apologize for including it. It induces wrath
in water-gardeners everywhere. Crews of volunteers
uproot and burn the plants from marshes in Minnesota.

Like most remedies of revisionists, it did the job
too well. Like kudzu, or hybrid trout, or anything introduced
with good intentions, it wipes out the competition.
Where it grows best it is least desired.
You can't buy it in any nursery. It seeds itself.

Doing their enterprising best, the spikes drive out
local weedy growth, what fits, what came first.
Best named of all wild things, for those who love the names,
it cast itself into the swamps and will not quit.
Now like an imperialist it has changed the landscape forever.

Distance

J I M   S I M M E R M A N

Everyone knows what the shortest distance
between two points is. And everyone knows how
there's an infinite number of points in between.

Imagine applying Zeno's Paradox to the phone company:
none of your calls would ever get through, but then
you wouldn't get billed for them either.

It's like trying to decide whether the glass
is half-empty or half-full when you'd just
as soon throw it back and pour another.

But the point is, sometimes you *have* to decide—
like pitching to the clean-up hitter:
Slider? Curve ball? Power against power?

And when the ball thumps off the bat—it's timing—
a good outfielder can tell *just by the sound*
which way to run, and how far, and how fast.

And the fans shoot straight up out of their seats
without thinking how knees are supposed to work,
and their shouts converge like a connect-the-dots puzzle.

Imagine yourself driving back from the game—
you're a little exhilarated and a little bored
and there's nothing, really, waiting at home

so you decide to meander, your car a duck
doing a cursive duck-glide down a road
that shimmers in the heat like a river.

Maybe the road runs next to a river.
You park, take off your shoes and socks,
roll up your pants and wade on out,

just standing there while the sky goes dark—
just standing there till you really can't say
where your body ends and the water begins;

or how the day got so quickly away;
or when the first grain of starlight appeared;
or whether your life's half-empty,

half-over, half-hearted, or just poorly timed.
Imagine yourself trying to come to the point
from such distance and so out of line.

Lonely Games

DAVID   EVANS,   JR.

In the lonely games
no one sees
the wonderful things you do,
or how well.

You sneak
into a barren stadium
during a warm, southerly wind
with a stack of special Frisbees.

You poise yourself
at the upwind endzone
looking downwind
to the distant uprights.

You want an audience
but it doesn't exist.
You make a dozen hundred yard
"field goals" and only the wind cheers.

A big gust comes up
and you're ready. You time it
perfectly and know damn well
when that thing landed in the upper seats

it was still rising.
It was still rising!
And as you shout it out
and look about, furious,

a roar of wind snaps out
your breath and hurries it
through all the empty seats
and sunburned confetti.

Play

ANN TOWNSEND

I want to play tough, beating my brother
at the game he loves, forcing the ball

over the net, a clean slice, so it sprays
the court's clay to sting against his legs,

ball skidding low, impossible to hit back.
I want that winner, so when the ball won't come

my way I swear, I throw my racquet when both serves
bounce free of their boundary lines.

The ladies on the next court are startled;
they signal a message with raised eyebrows, meaning both

what bad manners and *why get so excited.*
We play every good day this summer, our lives

suspended between college and home.
Our limbo spends itself in long rallies,

our bodies' feast of perfect coordination ruined
when we think too much, when we understand

the arm's appended power. The ball rushes by,
slamming into the backboard behind me.

I want to forget that failure and the racquet
I hold in my hand, to forget where I am,

to know only the surge of anger; this ball is mine,
I want to send it, to hit the sweet spot, to sail clean.

Why I Quit Dancing Lessons

GARY GILDNER

It wasn't riding the bus across town, eyeing my feet
& sweating too much, already pressing the wet
woolly back of tall Nancy McLeod
around the furnace, around the teacher's wheezing
cocker watching me butcher the cha-cha, & cross-eyed
Lester Deering screaming Why is your face so red!
No, it was the bluegills biting like crazy & Dirty Fred
smack in the middle, barefoot, laughing his skinned head purple.

Live Studio Wrestling

J I M   H A L L

The Murfreesboro Mauler peels
John Blank out of the ropes, where
he threw him,
and body slams him.
They ride together on the mat
like that for several minutes,
flipping like fish, the Mauler
grinding salt into John Blank's eyes.

They struggle to their feet
like rapist and rapee, Blank blinking
and blanching, the Mauler, mauling,
when a huge man from the studio audience
with sinking ships on his forearms
pops a packet of ketchup in his mouth
and leaps into the ring,
appalling the Mauler and drawing applause.
He goes for the villain

who steps aside neatly and plants a fist
in the ostensible tourist's throat.
The ketchup breaks open,
the fans at home slap their knees,
and the announcer stumbles on the word *hemorrhaging*
The camera spins around, simulating chaos.
And for a second we glimpse
a policeman lighting his cigarette
and a ten year old boy dragging
his bawling brother back from the bathroom.

Wrestling to Lose

GEOF HEWITT

None of us were winners, like
Armentrout or Beebe, the heavyweight
who surprised opponents twice his size
in the Unlimited Division, flipping one
who still scowled from the peevish handshake
that had to start each match.

Spring Weekend my parents drove my date up from New Jersey
and I wrestled the 135 pounder from Peddie
who took 30 seconds to pin me Spring Weekend
the year before. My father
clapped my back in the locker room
and pronounced it "a moral victory."

Behind the gym two weeks later
the hacks on the team smoked their first cigarettes
since fall and chafed at the gung hoes
who were still running laps. Where are they now?
Well, Armentrout's big in business for sure,
and Beebe's a famous neurosurgeon!

And us hackers? I'll hazard our wages
per capita can't touch *theirs*. We were artists,
idealists, the boys who invented wrestling to lose:
slam yourself down on the mat. With shoulders flat
hold your opponent just three seconds over you
helpless in the victory pose.

Ice Hockey

JONATHAN HOLDEN

Silver Lake has changed into a milky,
marble floor. Wind from around the bend
drives white dust up-ice with long broom-
strokes toward the dam. The lake
talks, mutters to itself as I take
my naked fingers out into air,
grab the laces, wind them round
my ankles, winch them so tight that my feet
wilt, then work back into my gloves.
I'm done: my fingertips are stones.
I lean, then, launch out over my stick
against the wall of the wind, make the whole
map of ice begin to move, the lightning-
splits of cracks begin to move
toward me, the sleek curves of other
skaters—etched with ice-spray where
their blades bit—begin to bend like moving
rails as the network of the city thins
to a few arcs across dark wilderness
where bubbles—the unblinking eyes
of fish—come flowing by. A loose
puck wobbles over the ripples.
I interrupt it, weave it with my wand,
let the wind into my lap to make me
stall, then with a willow flick
skim it back to the distant game,
follow it and join. The lake
begins to turn, a white wheel always
revolving, my legs robots, automatic,
kicking against the wheel
to make it spin until it streams so
fast my feet can't keep up, the wheel
flies out from under me, I sit down

hard on this slick seat that sears
my behind as it hisses to a halt,
then rise, chase down the game again,
thrust in my stick, grapple in the clatter.
The puck squirts free—in front of me—
alone, this rare coin, all mine.
I coddle it, nick the wheel, heave
at the wheel until it's whirling
under me in streaks, the goal swinging
into range, slap, miss, watch the puck
whiz, three guys stabbing after it
as I lean away into the force of ice
and level out, let the wind hit me
in the back and hurl me home again
across the fleeing map.

Coach Goes down the Hall Wondering Where All the Men Went

JACK RIDL

Where are they, for Christ's sake,
Coach wonders as he passes
what used to pass for men
slouched against the row of lockers,
gazing. What do they think about?
Suddenly, he feels as if he wants
to punch one, ram him up against a locker,
jam him inside, slam the door, spin the lock
to a code impossible to crack.
His short hair burns. His years of bending over math
and dribbling with his lame left hand
turn to stone. What do they do? They smoke,
plan ways to escape the very things

he dreamed of. What the hell
went wrong! Dribbling mattered. So did math.
So did the nights spent cramming for the credits
he would need to hold his job,
his place in class and on the bench.
But them? What do they want? Nothing?
He shakes his head, and when he
sucks in his gut, he feels
the awful smirk behind him, feels
the urge to throw an elbow, trip
anyone driving for the hoop.

Karate

J O N A T H A N   H O L D E N

Mel Brown was teaching us
logic: First soften your opponent.
Seize the hair like a housewife
snapping lint from a rug and
snap. Or break one arm, blind him
with the splinters of his own
nose and so make him available
for the greater mechanical advantage
of both your elbows,
the next link in an argument
leading straight to the mat.
Mel checked us again.
A welterweight, he was forged
like a wedge, perfect.
On the glistening basalt of his chest
you'd break your fist.
                  Daintily
as some finicky high-
fashion photographer coaxing

a girl's surly chin,
cajoling, tilting her head by
fingertip to hold a pose,
he retouched our stances, adjusted
my knee, my drooping
elbows, the tickling flatteries
of his attentions pleasant
as the fussings of a barber.
Satisfied, he stepped
back. He was, as that saying goes,
undressing us with his eyes,
and he was snapping
our pictures.

The Rodeo Fool

WALTER McDONALD

We hummed sad country songs all summer,
certain the bulls we shoved were worth it.
Nothing thrills a family crowd more
than a cowboy falling, even the king
of the cowboys, and one or two hurt bad
each night. They know riding bulls is brave
and crazy. They like a good stomping,
when rodeo clowns help them die laughing
in the face of danger, a black
two-thousand-pound bull pawing dirt,

goring the cowboy over and over. They scream
so loud they can't hear the screams
of the cowboy. I run out waving my arms
like an angel in makeup and baggy pants,
slam into the bull's broad butt,

grab his tail and twist and twist. The bull
stops goring and lifts his horns.
I'm wiping my hands up and down my pants
hung by suspenders up to my nipples,
like rubber waders Baptist preachers wear.
The bull looks back, stupid on all four
massive legs. The crowd loves it,

safe in the stands, munching beer nuts
and guzzling. I twist the tail till it burns,
drop it and wipe my hands three times
and make a face, then fake a double-take
at the bull's black eyes deciding
by god to kill me. I run,
hoping my aim for the rubber barrel
is better than it was two years ago.
By now, Jay or Billy Ray has dragged
the rider to safety and runs out
baiting the bull. The bull snorts,
swinging his head between us, tail limp,
testicles drooping like a water balloon.

The fool's baggy pants and derby
are a good costume to hide the blood
if the bull's tail-wise and quick
to gore anyone messing with his butt.
No one at rodeos pays to see clowns suffer,
clowns make it fun to watch a grown man
gored and stomped on by a beast. It can't be
bad as it seems if a fool in baggy pants
can shove a bull and crank his tail
and live. Even when we're gored,
bleeding inside our baggy pants,
ribs crushed, unable to breathe,

we pull ourselves up and double over,
bowing. We go on making believe it's fun
all the way from the arena:
it's in the rules. I couldn't say how many
stitches and crushed ribs, how many bones
Jay and Billy Ray and I have broken
and grown back. They couldn't pay me
enough to do this, if friends didn't grin
and raise a hand when we lift them
into the ambulance. People leaving

laugh at me and wave as if I'm some kind
of saint, a fool holy enough to do what
they'd like to do, nightly to save someone
from death and make believe it's fun.
My stupid moves prove nothing wild
is as wise and dangerous as men.
Because of me, they ride home humming,
not troubled by tons of metal hurtling
past their bumpers, believing death's a black bull
mad and charging, all men are brave and cunning,
that all fall down, get gored and trampled on,
all men are able to rise with the help
of clowns, able to look death in the eye,
to wear a clown's face, laughing, and walk again.

Challenge

SAMUEL HAZO

Leveling his pole like some quixotic lance,
trotting, trotting faster, faster to his mark,
slotting the pole, twisting upward to a bar,
contortioning clear, the vaulter drops in sand.

He wipes his hands and stumbles from the pit
with sand still sweated to his thighs and calves,
retrieves the pole and drags it like a mast
behind him down the cinder aisle, and waits.

I feel in my onlooker's hands the taped
and heavy barrel of the vaulter's pole
and see the bar notched higher for his leap.
His spikes clench earth, and all my muscles pull
to face a task with nothing but my skill
and struggle for the mark I must excel.

Tom Lonehill (1940–1956)

DAVID ALLAN EVANS

Opposed to crewcuts and buddies,
his black hair slick as grackles,
his black belt silver studded,
Tom Lonehill hid on his porch all day
behind thick eyebrows watching us.

He saw nothing good about slamming
a bamboo pole into a box and clearing
a ten-foot bar and falling back
down into heaped sawdust;
or smacking a baseball on the roof
of Woodrow Wilson Junior High;
or place-kicking a football over
a sagging telephone wire;
or shuffling spread-legged and
holding a beam of light underground
through the cool sewers of summer.

The rest of us made it, taking
a diploma, a wife, and a job and
settling down as our fathers before.
Now we tell our sons about baseball
and football and falling back into
sawdust and steering a beam of light
through the blind sewers.

But none of us explain Tom Lonehill—
how he hid on his porch all day behind
his eyebrows, how in the county jail
leaping from his cot he hanged himself
with his belt in the middle of a night
in July in the middle of his 16th summer.

I Hear the River Call My Name

S H E R Y L   L .   N E L M S

I've been fighting
them all

the bridge rail
the cement pillars
the bottomless gully

and the river

so smooth
and black
and deep

rolling along
down there through the night

calling to me

telling me
how easy it
would be

to stop
right here
and slip
in

The Suicide's Father

B A R O N   W O R M S E R

Everything has become a museum.
Where I live is where I lived.
My face in the mirror in the morning
Was my face. I am here the way a chair
Or painting is here. I have weight and
A meaning I cannot possess.

We walked to the war plaza, bought bags
Of popcorn, watched the jugglers and mimes,
Walked home through the lamp-lit twilight.
It was a Sunday in early spring.

What do you do when the past is
No longer yours? I was a simple man.
I thought it was something that could not
Be taken away. I would have it
For always. But I have lost it.

Now in those looks, excursions, mornings—
Even in laughter—I see death.
It is wrong but that is what I see.

I have put my purposes in a bag
And thrown them into a river and watched
Them sink. It did not take long.
It is cold in that river and now when I walk
I wander like a tramp or a bored pensioner.
People avoid me or babble courteously.

You, my boy, are never mentioned.
Of course, that is for the best. I have
Committed a crime, but I am not sure
What it was. It is a crime where there
Are no police or reports or even lies.

It is a crime of meals, gifts,
Postcards, worries, lullabies.

There was the time you asked for money.
The time I didn't hear from you for months.
But we all have those times and we live
And however battered we come around.

You did not like illusions. I do not think
You liked those grimacing mimes.
I, as a father, did. I did
What a father does. I talked about you.
My son was this, my son was that.
My son built little wooden planes
That really flew. I was proud. Like the mime
Who could not open the imaginary door, you frowned.

You were in the river for a week
Before they found what they said was you.
I had to say it too.
On what was a hand was a ring.

What was there before this to ever
Think twice about? Everything. Everything.

Pulling Peter Back

CHRISTINE HEMP

Since you died I try to pull you back
through the dovetailed joints in the
white pine toolbox you made for me,
hoping you'll slip from between the cracks.

And every time I cut a board
I measure twice, pulling the rule
out to a bird's-mouth mark. I expect to see you
standing there to double-check.

But you're stubborn as the two-by-twelves
I haul from the stickered stack and lay out
for loading. You never suffered chaos gladly
and used a plumb bob to true your winter woodpiles.

Yes, I can wrench the rusty nails from a plank
of spruce, hear them squeak in the
claws of my hammer, but you won't come loose.
I tug at the chalk line, snap the blue string
across the roof to mark the shingles' path.
Would that you'd appear out of that familiar dust.

Since you've gone I can't stop pulling—
even the blade on the red Swiss knife I gave you
for your birthday—till I look down to see
the cut across my hand. And I let go.

No Woman Is Ever Prepared

DEBORAH BOSLEY

The day after her mother died
she baked bread
taking fresh loaves
like long bones from the oven.

Vacuuming the carpet
she felt the suck of ashes
and later washing dishes
she let the greasy water
slip like a baby sliding
into life over her hands.

She washed windows
scouring the corners
free of wilting webs
then cleaned the refrigerator
discarding decayed food
collapsed into misbegotten shapes.

Three loads of laundry
she dumped on her bed
and fell into the heap
of twisted white sheets
rubbing her face
with her mother's slip.

Thinking about Bill, Dead of AIDS

MILLER WILLIAMS

We did not know the first thing about
how blood surrenders to even the smallest threat
when old allergies turn inside out,

the body rescinding all its normal orders
to all defenders of flesh, betraying the head,
pulling its guards back from all its borders.

Thinking of friends afraid to shake your hand,
we think of your hand shaking, your mouth set,
your eyes drained of any reprimand.

Loving, we kissed you, partly to persuade
both you and us, seeing what eyes had said,
that we were loving and were not afraid.

If we had had more, we would have given more.
As it was we stood next to your bed,
stopping, though, to set our smiles at the door.

Not because we were less sure at the last.
Only because, not knowing anything yet,
we didn't know what look would hurt you least.

The Enticing Lane

CHRISTOPHER   HEWITT

If I should be told,
suddenly and quite unceremoniously,
that I too had
The Disease and would be taken
from all this,
I would think over the years,
I had complained too much—
the phone's ringing constantly
(lucky I was to have
so many friends),
the hours of my job
(fortunate I was to have
a job I liked),
the lover leaving
(ah, but he was here,
wasn't he, and in my arms
for so long?).

I should have lived in
the moment, kept a secret
corner for myself to breathe in,
allowed my life to blossom
at last—each leaf uncurling
wet with secrecy to dry
in the spring air.
I should have taken more risks—
old stick-in-the-mud that I am—
a balloon trip over the estuary;
speaking up on behalf of the
deaf-mute man at the bank who
was so rudely abused by the teller;
that antique bowl with red
peonies on it that I could
have bought in a shop in England.
But I let myself be dissuaded
by the sensible people.
I should have sought more balance—
silence/laughter,
cool shadow/hot rain,
nights drunk on someone/nights
alone with the dark's quiet watching.
I should have followed intuition
to the nth degree and trusted it,
kept to that singular path, the enticing
lane with plush hedges, ripe fruit
and wafting scents that is always there
in the heart's eye and I could have
walked it, always prepared,
even into Death's Unknown and
still have been content, peaceful
as a child dawndreaming by open windows
before the others are up and everyone,
even the child, is wrenched into the world's
bombardment, the maelstrom of appointments
which constitutes a life.

Identifying Things

WENDY BARKER

Is diabetes catching, he asks,
middle-school braggadocio edged
this time with something else, I can't
quite put my finger on it,
until he tells about the needle,
that kid Jamie, jabbing a needle he had picked up
on the street, punctured far into the flesh
of my son's palm.

Trouble boils a greasy steam into the air.
Whose needle, what kind, whose veins
had it entered? My son, my son, only eleven
years old and the doctor over the phone doesn't help,
his nurse says you bet, plenty to worry about,
and it's not just AIDS we'd want to run tests for,
there's hepatitis, three strains now—find the needle,
bring in the needle, make sure those boys
find that needle.

       Under the oaks
a new kind of bird flocks at the feeder,
I have no idea what they are, they swarm
and dart around the perches, on the ground,
they are everywhere, and outside their shrill
wheezing chokes out the drone of trucks on the interstate.

So he will teach us death, perhaps.
We will allow him the perfect death.
We will all work on dying
together, we will give him that, and maybe
it won't even happen, maybe the needle
belonged to Jamie, he's a diabetic,
maybe it was just one of his own insulin needles,

probably there is nothing in the world
to worry about, chances are slim, we mustn't
upset our boy, mustn't blow this out
of proportion.

        I can't identify
the birds. They are too streaked
for goldfinches, they could be
warblers, winter plumage, but their beaks
are a little thicker, I'm just not sure
and none of these walls
line up straight.

When the boys find the needle and take it
to the principal and you stop by school
our kid is most upset because his father
is actually seen by his friends, only nerds have
parents who enter this territory,
he will never live it down, his own father
picking him up in front of his friends,
driving him to the doctor's. Just a little needle,
the kind for pricking a finger for small
blood samples, adults always overreact.
The doctor and the nurses laugh out loud,
at home the walls rise crisp
to the ceiling where the light dances.

        And the new birds
are pine siskins, yes, they are,
just a little yellow on the wings and tail,
it helps, it always helps when you know
what things are.

For Poppa, Asleep in the Smithtown Madhouse

PETER SERCHUK

When they knew you were sick
you drove yourself nuts. Chasing nurses
for crazy laughs, chewing through ashtrays
just to prove you were insane.
Hardening of the arteries, they said.
You squealed your approval
tugging at your open fly.

Lonely Ruth who washed her hair with beer
said you chased her into the bathroom.
Maybe she hated you for being the father
of her husband who was the father of her sons.
Maybe she hated the disease of men, her mother dying
and her own father in the streets with his linens and his ladies.
No matter. She washed and washed but the pain wouldn't rinse.
You son of a bitch stay away from me, she screamed.
Some days you were there other days you were sleeping.
This day your stomach growled. Your idiot hunger
pressed hard against the door.

The year was 1955
and what you needed Poppa was a good guess.
Every lawn was green with fluoride
and heaven so close we all begged to die.
At Smithtown you said it's better this way
but you were talking to the moon, talking to the blue face
of a young wife a million years ago.
Later, starving yourself to pneumonia
you cried, *No more, no more.*
I don't want to dream.

Oh Poppa, Poppa, bless me a voice.
I'm living with my own dreams now, clutching
wind through grass as if something could be saved.
I'm exhausted by the stubborn tick of possibility.
Still, when I take a deep breath from the fog of your face,
see your gray cap floating like a windy cloud
it somehow seems right despite this madhouse.
Even riding in that old Nash one last time
you forgave them, didn't you?
A giant hand reached to tousle my hair
while I held my tears like a little man.
That wind I'm clutching says you forgave me too.

The Old Man & His Calf

KEITH WILSON

. . . that he'll never sell, though
he bought it for market. Each
day, he postpones the day, the calf
grown to bull, he yanks and tugs
him down the meadow, cursing
affectionately, buying more
and more feed

it is the same with
the five chickens, and the goat
called Eleanor who ate his only
hat . . . "One of these days!"
he says

and eats his saltpork beans
with a rusty spoon, the whole bunch
of animals, fat, grazing, pecking
peacefully all around his shack.

Old Red

KATHLEEN IDDINGS

Any cow with half a brain could see
the clover over there was thicker,
had more buttony tops than her thinning pastures.

She'd leap the barbed wire,
suffer electric shock and torn teats
to get what she wanted.

It always ended in a huge bellyache,
the shredded udder which took weeks to heal.
Every time Grandpa pulled her blood-stained milk
she'd rip her kickers off,
thump his bucket over
or kick him in the leg.

"Goddamned cow never learns," he'd yell
and hit her with his three-legged stool.
She'd dance, pull at her chain, and wonder for a while
if it was all worth it.

The tenth time she jumped the fence,
Grandpa grabbed the double-barrel,
aimed at old Red and squeezed.

Buckshot hit her in the eye,
moaned her to her knees,
but Grandpa swore to hell he'd kill her
if she jumped the fence again.

It took the fire out of old Red.
Now while Grandpa eases milk from her battle scars
Red just stands there with her one eye,
ruminating over green corn and purple clover
just beyond the barbed wire.

i'll never

TODD MOORE

understand why
thompson didn't
shoot that big
timber wolf down
by dead prophet
creek he had it
nailed to the
crosshairs of
his sniper's
scope i cd feel
that greasy rifle
steel lean into
my finger & wanted
to swim inside
the embrace of
man & gun but he
wdn't fire when
he used the rifle
to look away i
knew it was
over except for
the sound of
wind in the
grass then he
levered the
shell & gave it
to me didn't you
hear it he asked
hear what
thompson smiled
the wolf was
singing

Leaving

J U D I T H   W .   S T E I N B E R G H

Our parakeet escaped from the house on the highest day
of spring. Birds across the country warbled with joy.
After the cold winter, after the cramped days inside
its cage or clasped in the hot hands of my daughter
who loved it even more than her bear, our bird knew
this was the day it had to go. For one second the cage
door and the front door were open. That bird streaked
out, made a sharp right across the porch, made another
sharp right (it was used to flying at right angles
from room to room) and flew up through the kitchen
lilac, skimmed the apple frothing with blooms, into
the highest boughs of the silver maple. Paula!
I screamed, leaping into the air like Nureyev, in some
wild hope I could catch her before she left. The fact
of my daughter's loss rose up and stuck. One side of my
heart broke, and the other sped off with the bird
on the most glorious day of her life. High, high
above us, a tiny blue kite streaming across the sky,
barely distinguishable from heaven.

How to Take a Walk

L E O   D A N G E L

This is farming country.
The neighbors will believe
you are crazy
if you take a walk
just to think and be alone.
So carry a shotgun
and walk the fence line.

Pretend you are hunting
and your walking will not
arouse suspicion.
But don't forget
to load the shotgun.
They will know
if your gun is empty.
Stop occasionally.
Cock your head and listen
to the doves you never see.
Part the tall weeds
with your hand and inspect
the ground.
Sniff the air as a hunter would.
(That wonderful smell
of sweet clover is a bonus.)
Soon you will forget
the gun in your hands,
but remember, someone
may be watching.
If you hear beating wings
and see the bronze flash
of something flying up,
you will have to shoot it.

Burying

PAUL RUFFIN

I found him stumbling about when the mother
died, an otherwise healthy calf, and fed him
by bottle until another cow came due, then
moved him in with her for suckling.
Third night she broke his neck.
It was a right and natural thing to do:

She reasoned her milk was for hers alone.
I found him barely breathing, head thrown
back, unable to rise for the bottle,
his eyes already hazing over; I could see
myself fading in them, backing into fog.
I brought the pipe down hard, twice, the
second time in malice: not for him or her,
but for the simple nature of things.
Blood came from his nose, his body
quivered. I dragged him from the barn.

The hole in the winter garden was easy, quick,
and the calf fit properly; but when the
first shovel of dirt struck his side,
he kicked, with vigor. I watched the flailing
foot strike against air. Nothing else moved.
There were no considerations: I did what
needed to be done. A few more scoops clamped
the leg and the earth stilled. I mounded
the grave and turned away, looking back once
to see that nothing heaved. I felt neither
fear nor sorrow, love nor hate. I felt
the slick handle of the shovel, slid
my thumb over its bright steel blade,
breathed deep the sharp and necessary air.

Killing the Dog

ROBERT MORGAN

Hoping he'll get run over, go off
on his own and die out of sight,
you put it off, can let no one else
do the amputation.
One of his eyes is a half

opened oyster, the other has the glaze
of infinity. He's deaf, no sense
of direction, control
of bowels or bladder. Goes everyday
shitting on doorsteps, stops traffic.

Strokes have burned off acres
of memory, bridges washed out. He's no
longer yours, but knows and backs
crippled when you come to kill.
Follow hating him for cheating

you of grace through snakey fields,
chiggers, through goldenrod, sweating
for a good shot, but he's gone.
Like when he ruined trout pools
you'd spent half an hour approaching

by diving in and thrashing downstream.
The running and anger make it easy. Find
him trembling, treed for
once by you and by age.
The shot heals but does not assuage.

Confession, Curse and Prayer

PAUL ZIMMER

for Justine

I confess all creatures I have killed:
Flies, mosquitoes, roaches, ants in number;
Sowbugs, moths, grasshoppers, and bees;
Also beetles, snails, spiders to less degree;
Then two snakes, a quail, four frogs,

One baby robin and a rabbit stoned
In a seizure of youthful cruelty;
Two mangled woodchucks and a dying cat in mercy;
Many fish, some crabs, once a chicken,
Toads, worms and a butterfly or two.
Thus I am steeped in death like any man.

I recall so many of their resignations:
The first shock and brief fluttering,
The eyes turning slowly into themselves,
Or the small shell suddenly crushed
While the limbs still twitch and clutch
At the final glimmers of perception,
At the irretrievable thing that is gone;
And I am guilty of these destructions.

God damn the man who calls this sentimentality!
Who could not think of these things
Without praying for a quiet mind?
Let nothing cruel stir in my blood again.

Ineffable Beauty

JAMES STRECKER

To create
the pigment of

roses

for your cheek,

living rabbits
were

tortured
in a lab; their

eyes were
burned away.

I have no word
to compare

your skin

to petals.

Waiting for the Splash

Last night
after you hung up
I wrote you a poem
hoping it might change your heart.

This morning I tell myself:
Get serious, man.
Someone once compared
writing a poem
and hoping it will
change the world
to dropping rose petals
down a deep well

waiting for the splash

To an Estranged Wife

August, another year and the same
sour air rises from the fallen fruit.
The days are too hot without the morning
fog to cool and subdue us; we agonize
with the birds and, like them, keep moving.
I cannot trust myself in this weather.
The air suffocates and the fruit trees
bend from their trunks and seem
to melt in the heat.
I listen to the birds and can make
no sense of it. It is another burden,
something I cannot keep or hold.

I think of the cold, of December,
when the little we believe we possess seems
lost to us. Indoors, I break the seal
on the mason jars and there comes to me
everything retrievable of summer:
the tender meat of the fruit, spices and
the succulent air like steam on the window,
your body, still here, leaning gently
against the cupboard doors.

Even When

CHRISTINE HEMP

I close my eyes
    the light that was
        you
            burns
                against my lids.

He Attempts to Love His Neighbors

ALDEN NOWLAN

My neighbors do not wish to be loved.
They have made it clear that they prefer to
        go peacefully
about their business and want me to do the same.
This ought not to surprise me as it does;
I ought to know by now that most people have a
        hundred things
they would rather do than have me love them.

There is television, for instance; the truth
    is that almost everybody,
given the choice between being loved and
    watching TV,
would choose the latter. Love interrupts
    dinner,
interferes with mowing the lawn, washing
    the car,
or walking the dog. Love is a telephone
    ringing or a doorbell
waking you moments after you've finally
    succeeded in getting to sleep.

So we must be careful, those of us who were
    born with
the wrong number of fingers or the gift
of loving; we must do our best to behave
like normal members of society and not make
    nuisances
of ourselves; otherwise it could go hard
    with us.
It is better to bite back your tears,
    swallow your laughter,
and learn to fake the mildly self-depreciating
    titter
favored by the bourgeoisie
than to be left entirely alone, as you will be,
if your disconformity embarrasses
your neighbors; I wish I didn't keep forgetting
    that.

When Leland Left Elma

R E E   Y O U N G

Elma called it witchcraft. I say
it's hard fact and everyday plain
as a pot going black from being set
too near the fire. It's men-and-
women stuff what made Leland
leave his wife for that hot-eyed
Jenny Stevens. Elma thinks the sun
shines brighter on Leland than
on anyone else, but I can tell you,
he was never a saint nor even
mildly resembled one. A year or so
past, when heavy rains washed out
the road at Sand Creek's bend,
I helped shovel mud. There
was Leland, smiling at me with
his pale eyes, finding reasons
to touch my arm, steady me
over the slickest places. Rain
had stuck my shirt front tight
across me and my jeans were
wet and shiny. Leland damn-near
licked his lips when he said,
"Let me assist you, honey."
There's not much truth in how Jenny
led him on, twisted his loyal heart
with lies. She just wanted his turkey
farm and safety, her so close to 48
and still single. Why, Elma
has as much curve and sway, holds it
as pretty, too, but an old meal's
forgotten when some quickie new
dish shows up on the table. No,
it wasn't a thing to do with magic.

Won't call it such either and let
that rutting buck pretend there was
something special in what him
and Jenny did. It's nothing
but a pot turning black. Pots
can turn rusty right soon after that.

The View

PHILIP SCHULTZ

Remember how the door in our first apartment always stuck?
Now the building is a Chinese laundry & the Spaniard,
who kept us up clapping flamenco, asked where you were.

I admitted I didn't know. Perhaps too much happens
& the loss is finally for something that never existed?
Returning may be a step forward, but now the question

is how much we can bear to question. Change, I think,
happens almost always too late. Yes, I still miss
the way you washed your hands before undressing & how

your green eyes darkened with desire. I remember
what was promised. That once I believed I could die of love.
That, like fate & youth & weather, it continued forever.

This is the first day of the new year & around me everywhere
the light is less convincing. I mean to say the view this morning
from every direction is still lovely, if a little darker.

Talking Long Distance
after One A.M.

MARY CLARK

On the telephone, breaking up
again, I was doing great—
sticking to my point based firmly
in facts she could never argue
her way out of; recalling
certain horrors between us,
which she refused to remember;
enumerating our differences;
not wavering once from her
soft suggestions whispered repeatedly,
as if none of what I said mattered

—until she mentioned her legs,
those legs. And I remembered
my fingers on them, and other
parts of my body on them.
There was something about her legs.
They resembled everything
about her: the way she made
breakfast in the morning,
grabbing right for the spoon
and holding it tight in her hand;
the way she'd cry immediately
at a great sadness, or laugh loud
when something was funny.
And in bed, she was everywhere,
and those legs were everywhere,
and fear went out the window
when she opened it.

Some loves are more body
than anything else. They make
the mind look shameful.

In the late evening
we would go out and sit
in our chairs on the porch.
The stars were something
to look at, not discuss.
She would lean back
and cross her legs
up on the railing,
and those legs were solid
as she was solid
in what she wanted.

The Two Orders of Love

E D W A R D   F I E L D

We have every right to hate them, he said,
looking at the girl nestling against the handsome head
of the blond giant in the row in front
of us sitting in our separate seats.
And sometimes it does seem
they have all the breaks.

In most places, outside the big cities,
even our men feel compelled to go with them—
you feel so out of it otherwise—
and except for a handful of rebellious young,
we shrink from contact with each other in public
as though by some repellent chemistry.

It is only fear.
If our longing could be expressed
we too would be hanging on each other's shoulders,
our lovers too would be profiled in doorways
and starred on the public grass of parks.

But for us it is forbidden,
not so much by law
as by a system of intimidation
not only of our actions but worse, of our feelings,
so that what we deny ourselves we persecute in others.

And they, our sisters, have the right
and are encouraged to enjoy
those empires of careless pleasure
we can only dream of, and pillage in haste, in secret,
or if we walk hand in hand, there is no ease in it.

We have every right to hate them and yet do not
because it is in its essence
a different thing we want, though it looks the same.
Nature needs both to do its work
and humankind, confusing two separate orders of love,
makes rules allowing only one kind
and defies the universe.

Gone Astray: Little Miss Muffet

DAVID JAMES

First of all,
the spider was not interested
in Miss Muffet.
In fact, he was engaged
to Sylvia Satwicks,
the long legged one
who lived in the rose bush.
No, there was no romance here.
Secondly,
he did not want the curds & whey.

He thought it was ghastly stuff,
too mushy, too blah,
too civilized for his taste.
The reason he came down
from the tree
& sat beside Little Miss Muffet,
the reason he shot his gossamer
& tightroped down to the tuffet
was because
he wanted to scare
the crap out of her!
She sat there day after day
eating her lunch,
believing herself to be God's gift
to the world,
stroking her own golden curls
& talking to the sky like a mirror.
He wanted to bounce around
making his ugliest face
& send that uppity bitch screaming,
wanted to see her dress flapping
around her waist as she ran,
for once
he wanted to be
the cause of something
big.

Help Is on the Way

HERBERT SCOTT

1 Frankenstein's Wife Writes to Ann Landers

Dear Ann, I think I am losing my husband.
He never straps me to the bed anymore
or fiddles with my parts.
I haven't had a charge in weeks.

Sometimes I think he wants to do me in.
There were intimations of this last week
when I found water in my oil can.
Am I going crazy?
I have faulty wiring and poor compression,
yet he won't fix anything around my body.
Lately, strange arms appeared beneath the couch,
and a leg under the table,
and teeth in my teacup.
I began to put things together.
And finally, last night, he robbed the grave
of that little tramp
who died down the street.
What shall I do?
Should I sever connections?
I would like to make this marriage work.
But where have I failed? I try to keep neat.
Heaven knows it's difficult with no help
in the kitchen, and nothing to wear,
and vapor lock to contend with.
I think I am pregnant, and he won't pay the bills.
What will I do when they turn off the lights?

2   Ann Landers Replies to Frankenstein's Wife

Listen Toots, I've had letters,
but this one takes the cookies.
You are one of a kind.
Did you ever stop to think
the fault may be yours?
You may not have much to work with
but there is no excuse for being run-down.
Shock him with a frilly new nightgown,
set a nice table. It's the little things that count.
Have you checked your breath lately?
Personal hygiene is the ticket, and he'll stop
playing footsie with that leg under the table.
Give the rooster a roost to crow about

and he'll send the other chickens home
is my motto. I don't really think
he is trying to do away with you.
If he does, see a lawyer. If he doesn't,
see a psychiatrist. You may need help.

The Visiting Paleontologist Feels Her Thigh

GRACE BAUER

Home, he is known
as a shy man, given
to minute analysis and quiet
evenings with his family in the den,
but here, he is taken
with the role attention gives him.

She hangs on every word
when he lectures on his digs
in the desert, his theories
of where we've come from
and how far along we've gone.

Afterwards, there are questions
and cocktails. He has too many
of both and by the time
she extends her hand in a simple
greeting, he takes
the gesture for much more
than it's meant; clings to her
slender fingers as if they were
a link he had just uncovered.

He notes the delicate slope
of her cheekbones, the firm
square set of her jaw, but misses
the flash of annoyance
in her eyes when he runs his free hand
down the curve of her spine
and lets it come to rest below
her hipbone as if it belonged.

She clears her throat, retreats
across the room to her lover
and wraps her arm around his waist,
hoping the evidence will convince
the man of science she knows
where true affection lies.

He observes the obvious
clues and blushes, then strikes up
a conversation on the Pleistocene Epoch
with a colleague who's eager to please,
and rambles on till the party's over
and she has left without speaking.
By tomorrow, he'll bury the memory
of his embarrassment and her name.
But tonight he sleeps in a stranger's bed
and dreams about the flesh that hides her bones.

After Quarreling

R. T. SMITH

Under clouds, I walk through lupine,
sumac, a stand of dying briars, to find
the new clearing where I have worked
all week cutting hickories for firewood

and the sun deck you asked for. I stumble
through debris slowly, trying to recall
your face, but there's too little light
to shape anything clearly, so I sit
on one stump clean as an altar to let
my eyes adjust. Through dark, I wonder
how long before oil from the chain saw
will seep completely underground, how
long before my sweat-scent is gone
and a herd of deer come here to paw
the earth for moss. I strive to see
a buck's antlers, the sleek profiles
of a dozen doe, but darkness again
intrudes. A mild wind reminds me
how your hair smells in the morning,
the feel of your sleep-warmed skin,
but sawdust scent dominates the air.
My fingers follow patterns on dry bark.
Surely only the owl can be nostalgic
for a forest at night, the quick rustle
of small beings in the brush. You
must be sleeping now by the settling fire,
as I rise to pace this circle of regret.
I wish the clouds would move away,
wish words that burned would change
to smoke and drift off. Hopefully, I
turn for home, seeking solace, and find
the moon underfoot, not lost at all,
a wedge of fresh wood carefully cut
to control the path of one tree's
fall. Tracing the grain, my hand can
feel the implicit light, the hickory
heart still moist with amber sap.
Perhaps I can carry this small gift
to complement a dying fire. Perhaps
I can walk back, wake you and apologize,

as wind gives the dense clouds direction
and mica bits in the cold road glow,
now that only half the moon is gone.

married 3 months

SHERYL L. NELMS

Walter always took
his bath
first

then sat in
the car
and honked

while Grace bathed

until
the day
Grace ran

a dripping wet
nude

to the car

The Belt Buckle

LEO DANGEL

There's no use putting it off, Audrey,
I'll tell you straight out,
I can't make myself wear
that belt buckle you gave me.

It isn't true that I have looked
for a belt worthy of that buckle.
I haven't been looking. Audrey,
you might have bought a buckle
with anything else on it, a lone star,
for instance. A horse, a sixgun,
a saddle, a boot, or even one of those
blue Indian stones. But you had to buy
a belt buckle with, of all things,
the Praying Hands. I know
your intentions were good, Audrey,
but didn't you stop and think
what those hands would be praying over?
A man wearing that buckle in bars,
sooner or later, would have to fight.
I ask you, Audrey, would Willie Nelson
wear such a buckle? I hate to hurt
your feelings, Audrey. Maybe
I could hang it on my truck dashboard.

Newlyweds

D A V I D   E V A N S ,   J R .

I have to watch my wife.
Don't get me wrong, I love her.
Still, I walk about on tiptoe
peeking around corners, over counters
to make sure she doesn't pluck
grizzled crumbs from the floor to eat.
I have to make sure there's no furry tuna
or rancid egg salad in the fridge.
God knows I love her.
But I swear she flirts with ptomaine.
I don't get much rest, but it's worth it.

Oh sure we're almost broke, I say, but
can't we please get rid of the rotten donuts?
She shakes her head. They're not that rotten.
And for God's sake, I say, that pork
is killing our air. Let it go, I say.
So you see how it goes?
Now I wouldn't come right out and say
that she's some carrion-hound
in the skin of a woman,
that wouldn't be fair, after all, I love her.
I don't know. Maybe
she's a risen Mithridates, eating
and drinking from the "many-venomed earth"
to build a powerful immune system
to rise above the poison in the world.
It's all unclear.
I won't know anything for a while.
But you see, my first impulse is to grab her hand
and stop it—to monitor each morsel of food
going into her mouth. She's my wife.
What is a husband, after all, if he can't protect
his wife from evil?
But then, what is a wife who lets it onto
her tongue?
So do you see why I stalk about in my own home?
What if I stumble on her sitting
in the kitchen one day, smiling, dunking
a bright blue slice of bread
into a cup of strychnine?

Anna Marie

PETER ORESICK

She has missed Mass again.
She fries pork for Sunday dinner
and her 7-year-old can see her halo
sucked into the exhaust fan.
The other kids wrestle in the den
while the oil sizzles.
The nerves of her breaded hands twitch.

                    At dinner
she hates how her husband chews
with an open mouth, breathing heavily.

By the time she's scoured the last pan
the kids are back from the alley shouting
about a dead pigeon
and how its body is opening out.
They want permission to bury it
in the rose bed, and she says okay,
just get out.

Her husband's already asleep
under the paper, the TV on,
his mouth open.
                    She stares for minutes
before poking him awake.

Gossip

JUDITH W. STEINBERGH

She was a mother you could count on. She was like the sun
and the moon, the seasons, the constellations, the orbit
of Saturn, the laws of gravity. She could cope. Everyone
took it for granted. She did this for years and years and
years until it was like breathing, like getting up, like blood
in the veins, and the husband came and went on the train
or the plane carrying a briefcase or a suitcase. He was a
footnote to the thesis of their lives. So when he left for the
West Coast for six weeks, everything seemed as it always
seemed, but back in the suburbs, she mailed the ticket to his
mother in Wales, painted the trim, took his shirts to the
cleaner, cooked a week of meals and froze them, booked
one passage on a freighter with no return, and four days
after her mother-in-law arrived and six days before her
husband was due home, she left it all behind, ruining in one
act a reputation it took her years to create, scandalizing
a community, stirring up worse than dust, leaving husbands
and wives sweating in their king-sized beds.

Appearances

PHIL HEY

deceive. Where is there school
to learn how suddenly and slightly
the history of love begins?
A door opening down the hall, then closing,
a candle lit, a silence or a word.
Such pale skin for the heart to beat beneath.

2

America,
it's hard to get
your attention

Patriotics

D A V I D   B A K E R

Yesterday a little girl got slapped to death by her daddy,
    out of work, alcoholic, and estranged two towns down river.
America, it's hard to get your attention politely.
    America, the beautiful night is about to blow up

and the cop who brought the man down with a shot to the chops
    is shaking hands, dribbling chaw across his sweaty shirt,
and pointing cars across the courthouse grass to park.
    It's the Big One one more time, July the 4th,

our country's perfect holiday, so direct a metaphor for war
    we shoot off bombs, launch rockets from Drano cans,
spray the streets and neighbors' yards with the machine-gun crack
    of fireworks, with rebel yells and beer. In short, we celebrate.

It's hard to believe. But so help the soul of Thomas Paine,
    the entire country must be here—the acned faces of neglect,
the halter-tops and ties, the bellies, badges, beehives,
    jacked-up cowboy boots, yes, the back-up singers of democracy

all gathered to brighten in unambiguous delight
    when we attack the calm and pointless sky. With terrifying vigor
the whistle-stop across the river will lob its smaller arsenal
    halfway back again. Some may be moved to tears.

We'll clean up fast, drive home slow, and tomorrow
    get back to work, those of us with jobs, convicting the others
in the back rooms of our courts and malls—yet what
    will be left of that one poor child, veteran of no war

but her family's own? The comfort of a welfare plot,
    a stalk of wilting prayers? Our fathers' dreams come true as
        nightmare.

So the first bomb blasts and echoes through the streets and shrubs:
    red, white, and blue sparks shower down, a plague

of patriotic bugs. Our thousand eyeballs burn aglow like punks.
    America, I'd swear I don't believe in you, but here I am,
and here you are, and here we stand again, agape.

When Bosses Sank Steel Islands

A L I C E   F U L T O N

in the North Sea, I was issued this survival
suit and hired to dive.
From the chopper I looked into towers
neat as watchworks, fortresses
with orange flares that roared
in gassy, dragonish glamour, with oily steel
stairs whose perforations distantly contained
the sea.

Here wind is unimpeded.
We speak of it in knots,
as if that measure could restrain it.
You have to trust
unsteady things: the sealant, the wet-
suit, the precision of the pressure
chamber. After deep work
I rest for days there, dreaming of sea

level, of leaves, of stone
croft ruins backlit by refinery
lights, rills of yellow
that waver against night like nonpareils or rainbows
in a spill, and black-
backed gulls drilling down
on newborn lambs. Food

and magazines slip through
a lock and music through a pipe. When needed,
a diving bell lowers me to bottom. There
I tend harvest in the dark.
I make sure pipelines
leave the stinger at good angles. I do
odd jobs, cut and join, move
obstacles. Some say a blowout would kill all

those birds with feathery names: the kittiwake, the guillemot,
puffins, murres . . . What can I do?
I know one prayer: send gushers
of sun glad as Boomtowns, send
a breather. I dive to live.
I stand on my survival, a small platform
above the fuel, the revenues. I dive for what
some call a god-
send: Black gold! The world's crude.

Out of the Mines

GARY YOUNG

We burn the coal in our lungs
with a slow fire.
Birch pipe,
anthracite
and the smoke pours out everywhere.

There is a black crescent under our nails,
a real moon,
the dark side.

Blue Collar

J O H N   M .   R O D E R I C K

Three shifts of weaving and cutting,
grinding and polishing,
washing in acid and buffing out burrs
Twenty four hours a day

Till the river runs black
and the sky sucks in stack smoke
and husbands and wives
meet in the parking lot
when her shift ends and his just begins:

"The kids're at your mother's
and Billy got a nosebleed
so don't faint when you see
the towel in the sink!"
And the presses fret down with a hiss
and steam pours from the cured rubber
and from his face
Twenty four hours a day

As he pulls hot tin-sheets
from the jaws of progress and
shakes rubber donuts into a barrel
waiting to be shipped
to another factory that needs rubber donuts
Twenty four hours a day

Where men on the night shift
catch moths the size of butterflies
in the reprieve of ten minutes down time
while the blades of their cutters are sharpened
and even the bricks of the building
sweat from the toil
Twenty four hours a day

Until the horn belches on Friday
for a weekend of rest
except there's time-and-a-half
on Saturday to get out the orders
so the company can make good
on his four cent raise
and the kid may need braces
so he eats alone in the kitchen
between back-to-back shifts
wondering if it's supper or breakfast
and the D J on the A M
calls for rain on Sunday

No Job

J I M   D A N I E L S

Laying off, they're laying off
softball teams swinging
their bats suddenly heavy
the ball so small.

A ton of robots in his dream
march across the field
men nervously put
out their cigars.

Tire tracks across his lawn
faded stripes, dead tiger
old soldier not sure
about the war, any war.

He drinks Mad Dog
he smokes homegrown
he sits naked with the want ads
he barks up the wrong tree.

He wants to skin himself
hang his hide out to dry
bugs, sticky dimes crawling on his arms
there's no jobs, no no no jobs.

He burns a cigarette
into the arm of his chair
his oldest child
his father, the sofa.

A woman shrinks his house
with a vacuum cleaner.
It's his wife
she sucks him up.

He sells his car, buys a junker
he sells his records, has a yard sale
he gets rid of his dog: tiny hairs
he'll never be gone.

Around the block he walks, sun
drying him out. Neighbors
his age, younger, older: raisins.
They nod, no jobs.

High school, toking behind auto shop
parking lot sticky in the heat.
Ford, Chevy, Chrysler—
where you gonna work?

Sweat darkens his shirt. He walks
home, drains a beer, sucking something
down at last. His father got him in: greasy
coveralls. Nice check. Car. Wife. House.

She cooks mac and cheese
she cooks dented cans
he goes for long walks
he never gets lost.

He pulls out
all the bushes in his yard
swinging a shovel at the roots.
He chases the paperboy.

Television smashed in the driveway.
His wife hides with neighbors.
No, no, no jobs:
he throws his knife in the air.

The Market Economy

MARGE PIERCY

Suppose some peddler offered
you can have a color TV
but your baby will be
born with a crooked spine;
you can have polyvinyl cups
and wash and wear
suits but it will cost
you your left lung
rotted with cancer; suppose
somebody offered you
a frozen precooked dinner
every night for ten years
but at the end
your colon dies
and then you do,
slowly and with much pain.

You get a house in the suburbs
but you work in a new plastics
factory and die at fifty-one
when your kidneys turn off.

But where else will you
work? where else can
you rent but Smog City?
The only houses for sale
are under the yellow sky.
You've been out of work for
a year and they're hiring
at the plastics factory.
Don't read the fine
print, there isn't any.

Bones in an African Cave

P E T E R   M E I N K E

Bones in an African cave
gave the show away:
they went violent to their grave
like us today.

Skulls scattered on the ground
broke to the brain;
the missing link is found
pointing to Cain.

Children in the street
pry up the cobblestones.
Old instincts repeat
in slender bones.

To my violent son,
beautiful and strong,
caps in his polished gun,
I hymn this song.

Grow tall and gay and wild,
strong-voiced and loud;
be proud of the fierce blood
that won't die out.

All things repeat
after the floods and flames:
new boys play in the streets
their ancient games.

House Keys

V I C C O C C I M I G L I O

Late at night when I walk home
I put my house keys between my fingers
making a jagged metal fist
to protect me from everything living.
Often, I imagine one of the jutting barbs
puncturing the shaded skin below the eye
and sawing against the eye socket,
but what good are a few keys facing a knife?

Yesterday, when I rode home on the bus,
the woman sitting across the aisle from me
slipped her house keys between her slender fingers
before she stepped into the six o'clock winter.
Watching her I felt cold inside,
and though that was also my stop I waited,
then walked back to my apartment
as all the locks in the city turned in my stomach.

wounds #13

S A F I Y A H E N D E R S O N – H O L M E S

she was there, on her
hands and knees when the

baby came, feet first
with eyes of an owl

and the fist her husband
hit her with

birthmarking its skin
no one cried

The Burnt Child

HERBERT SCOTT

I have no lips, no nose.
My mouth is a howl,
my tongue a choir.
No one can clap
my ears. I can

bite. Must I thank
God for my eyes? They
will not close.
The world spills
ceaselessly into them.

If I could have hair
or ears, or nose,
or eyes that close,
which would I choose?
None of those.

Lord, give me lips
to kiss this life.

Flames

RONALD WALLACE

We badgered him for days on the playground
as he grinned out from underneath his misery,
his shy resistance to our pleas
thick glasses we could hardly see through.
When he finally raised his trouser leg,
the cotton pajamas mysteriously underneath,
his red skin, blistering and squamous,
glistered with all our small imaginations could take.

He must have regretted it forever—
the fire of our eyes burning deeper than fire,
the ash of our cold avoidance after.
I should have known better—my own father
crippled past rage or approbation, everyone
politely going on about their lives,
or looking the other way—the slow burn of embarrassment,
how losses and disasters first attract,
but then repel us, all our carefree cells
shouting out at recess, *Not me! Not me!*
But he stood there in the corner like a ruined building
as we all ran away egging fat Joannie Conrath
to tackle the prettiest girls
and hold them down and hostage
for our hot lips to see.

Harold Iverson, Teacher

RODNEY TORRESON

whose stamp albums saved us
from Sunday school,
you gave us the gospel in stamps:
free issues of the Mackinac Bridge;
the Mercury project; the unused Kennedy
and his eternal flame.

But when your daughter was slain,
Harold, the stamps
we amassed: stamps of the
whirling Laundromat,
of her cloudy clothes basket
she carried to the car,
of her keys unlocking
the chromy night, stamps

of her killer hunching up
from the footwells
while she adjusted her breath
in the mirror.

We'd never visit you again.
My album grew dark with her face.
I buried it in the basement
where dampness glued the stamps
down into the years.

But they rise now,
fly up under my eyelids:
stamps of the ball field
in your final year,
your waving from your mailbox
across the street
while I shied away
to follow the ball.

Years later,
I flick that old mitt, my heart,
to catch you, hoping I can pull in
those years, Harold, pull you in
from across the street
where you always stand;
hoping in a stream of prayer
your clumsy hands would break
into letters of forgiveness
with ancient postage and script,
all the history of pardon
that preceded us,
that I would hold you, delicate man,
as the names of stamps
stuttered from my lips.

Sister

KATHLEEN IDDINGS

You still wake trembling
wild-eyed, watchful,
listening for Dad's approach.
So do I.

Older, you were conscripted first.
Introduced me to boot camp;
taught me to dodge shrapnel,
to run for the woods when missiles split the air
like belts on flesh.

We never knew why.
Our radar told us by the slam of a door
or the tone of his voice
when to take cover.

We wear purple hearts
but not on our lapels.
Our dreams tell us
we were too long at the firing line.

Recurrence

JANE WILSON JOYCE

In an old house
now a museum
the owner
stabbed his daughter's lover
to the heart
on the morning of their
wedding day
over a century ago.

The white silk dress,
sewn with her own hands,
never worn,
sealed in a glass cabinet,
stirs and sways on its hanger
once in every year.

After so long
my heart still sways
at sight, or fancied sight,
of you. Memory
swings round
in a face, a voice,
in the rasping of a hanger
hung on the back of a door
pulled shut.

What Holds Us Back

LIZ ROSENBERG

The great wall is crumbling
between East and West.
At the Bernauerstrasse, shoppers push out
where old women collapsed down worn bedsheet ropes.
Sunlight dissolves the iron curtain
like the veil rent at the temple gate,
the earth in its newness "without fence."
In Poland on May Day young women are weaving
ribbons up and down around the pole.
In China, by the gate at Tiananmen Square,
students lie under mounds of fresh dirt,
their faces still young, bones beautiful.

The Best Dance Hall
in Iuka, Mississippi

T H O M A S   J O H N S O N

Nothing's too good for the women
Of the Klan.
One by one
The records slot and spin

As they fan out over the dance floor
Like flies
On a bull pile,

Unaware that cut three to one
With the sawdust
Under their heels

Is that disappearance in shantytown
Of a young girl

From which their husbands
Have ground
Their complicity

To a fine, squaredance grit
Of powdered tooth
and bonemeal.

The Failures of Pacifism

R O N A L D   W A L L A C E

When our milk goats and their kids cavorted
into a dark nest of mud daubers camouflaged
in the high grass of August, and danced
their dance toward oblivion, their tough skins

a sizzle of ripple and twitch, their sweet
faces swollen, one eye cordoned off from
the other, one nostril Picasso-like, comic, askew,
their udders all elbows and knuckles,
precarious balloons,

                    my daughter,
the vegan, and animal rights activist, who,
like certain Tibetan monks or Hindus,
would sweep the path in front of her
as she walked so as not to step on
the least of this world's sweet creatures,
heartsick and outraged, surreptitiously
commandeered a large can of Raid
from the dark garden shed, and nuked
those ancient demons mercilessly,
dispatching them and their black offspring
to the scrutiny of history
and the land of kingdom come.

Why I'm in Favor
of a Nuclear Freeze

CHRISTOPHER   BUCKLEY

Because we were 18 and still wonderful in our bodies,
because Harry's father owned a ranch and we had
nothing better to do one Saturday, we went hunting
doves among the high oaks and almost wholly quiet air . . .
Traipsing the hills and deer paths for an hour,
we were ready when the first ones swooped—
and we took them down in smoke much like the planes
in the war films of our regimented youth.
                              Some were dead
and some knocked cold, and because he knew how
and I just couldn't, Harry went to each of them and,

with thumb and forefinger, almost tenderly, squeezed
the last air out of their slight necks.

Our jackets grew
heavy with birds and for a while we sat in the shade
thinking we were someone, talking a bit of girls—
who would "go," who wouldn't, how love would probably
always be beyond our reach . . . We even talked of the nuns
who terrified us with God and damnation. We both recalled
that first prize in art, the one pinned to the cork board
in front of class, was a sweet blond girl's drawing
of the fires and coals, the tortured souls of Purgatory.
Harry said he feared eternity until he was 17, and,
if he ever had kids, the last place they would go would be
a parochial school.

On our way to the car, having forgotten
which way the safety was off or on, I accidentally discharged
my borrowed 12 gauge, twice actually—one would have been Harry's
head if he were behind me, the other my foot, inches to the right.
We were almost back when something moved in the raw, dry grass,
and without thinking, and on the first twitch of two tall ears,
we together blew the ever-loving-Jesus out of a jack rabbit
until we couldn't tell fur from dust from blood . . .

Harry has
a family, two children as lovely as any will ever be—
he hasn't hunted in years . . . and that once was enough for me.
Anymore, a good day offers a moment's praise for the lizards
daring the road I run along, or it offers a dusk in which
yellow meadowlarks scrounge fields in the gray autumn light . . .
Harry and I are friends now almost 30 years, and the last time
we had dinner, I thought about that rabbit, not the doves
which we swore we would cook and eat, but that rabbit—
why the hell had we killed it so cold-heartedly? And I saw
that it was simply because we had the guns, because we could.

Why Is It

ROBERT A. FINK

at the half-price book table in the mall,
you always find picture histories of war
nobody buys but can't put down
like when you were a kid in the corner drug
reading comic books flopped on the bottom shelf
of the magazine stand, your dad sitting at the counter
buying a cherry Coke for some recent high school graduate
home on leave, first time, who just dropped by
the Rexall to parade his uniform?

You know what I mean
and why we can't believe this book—
too many piles of bodies, too many summary hangings
and bullets to the base of the brain
to trust the photographers.

Like the full-page spread
of the lovely Russian girl swinging from a rope
delicate as a necklace of pearls, her head
cocked to one side as if trying to catch
the flattering whisper passed across the aisle in school,
her boyfriend winking he'll meet her later in the grove—
certainly not to shoot at Germans, outside Minsk, October, 1941;
certainly not to find themselves hanged together in a barn
by curious soldiers who seem to want to touch
the girl's taut breast, smooth back her tousled hair,
even rub a finger along her full, protruding lower lip.

Shipping Out

JOAN LaBOMBARD

The sun glints on his weapon
And he is young to bear
That engine of blind chance
Like his old racket or a pair of skis
Slung easy on his shoulder.
He might be headed for the courts,
The playing courts, the courts of summer
Where tan, colt-legged girls frisk after him,
Or for the white ski slopes,
The musical long fall
Through space and out of time
Into the plummeting body of a bird.

Receive him gently as those tides
That turned his days and hours received him—
Gently, you winged ships,
As the crushed grass and the snow.

He might be bent
On a picnic or a Sunday's outing.
The rifle shouldered like a toy
And fitted to the outworn racket's crease,
Lies easy there, and sleeps
With the loaded dice
And the fixed game,
And the angel of death's indifferent wager laid.

Conscientious Objector

HENRY CARLILE

Through dust deepened by others
we practiced to be missed,
cursing, an olive-green flotsam,
venomous and terrified.

Through smoke from mock bombs,
through the flare's blue failing light,
like amputees on knees and elbows,
with M-1's crooked in our arms,

beneath thorns of barbed wire
and the stitched red lines of bullets
we rowed our flesh against earth
and made slow progress.

Then one more desperate than the rest
put up his hand and howled
and fell back clutching his wrist,
the rags where fingers had flexed.

We knew the truce would soon be signed.
Touch that had fathomed Preludes
protested to the dust. For what?
There will be other wars, he said.

Matthew Schnell

RODNEY TORRESON

In high school he quit them all:
the touchdowns tucked under his arm,
the lumbering grunts of his

teammates' praise, their slaphappy hands,
the cheerleaders' leaps and their awe.

Drafted, he couldn't leap one barrier
toward meaning. When he broke in close combat,
they sent him home, where he hid in the house,
eating darkness, weighing finally 400 lbs.

No and no, he'd say to me and lakes
of pole fishing. When at last he went,
his handshake slack as his castout line,
his conversation carried no hook.
Not a feature remained on his face.

For years his reflection floated the water.
Then last April, he mounted a tractor
in the backyard, steered into his
darkest thought. When his revolver
shined like the sun, he fired into his head,
reading the Bible between each blast.

Now every night his parents dream he
paddles a rowboat into their yard, pulling up
happiness oar to oar, through the wavy
grass, through all the years he sat and sat.
Through the army and every football game
played without him he comes paddling back
to the family fold, smiling, waving a hand now,
calling from the blue skies of his brain.

Hunting on the Homefront

B I L L   D O D D

I live in the Nez Perce country
a few yards from the village, Cove,
up a ridge to the primitive area
and good fishing if I hike
from the Mormon homestead, sturdy
but hard to warm in the Oregon winter
though wood is free at the mills.
So many pheasant I supply
an aunt with hat feathers,
and a deer hangs in the cellar downstairs
along with a ball of elk jerky;
ducks, I shoot off puddles
or the lip of the slough
as they jump from the river
or across the road at a gravel pit
where I once got a drake
then a cock getting up at the noise
while a small boy and his father
watched from a stand of elder
almost in the line of fire.

Afterwards, I stop at Cover Tavern,
sometimes talking to Lonesome Jack,
or the Sacajawea Hotel and Bar
amid the Vietnam debate,
particularly keen for the geographer
I hunt with at a small lake,
his two boys draft age,
who purposely never gets a duck
with the single-shot twenty-gauge.

One foggy afternoon, perfect for birds,
masked swans turning on the water,

he confides before he'll see
his sons go to slaughter,
he'll take them to sanctuary,
like Chief Joseph, into Canada.

War

KATHERINE SONIAT

My mother said he was real,
not a friend but my father,
home, finished with a war
as he snapped rubber bands
around each lobster's red claws
in that Boston apartment.
Helplessness was what he had
even before the salt poured
its shadowy stream into the kettle—
his lobsters wobbling an altered race
across the linoleum as he winked
and took my mother by the hand,

took me to the bedroom with the foldaway
cot. I sucked my thumb, stroked her satin slip
I kept for the dark, wishing it was dark.
He stood behind her with his big gold
bourbon glass, his breath moving
into her hair and out of her hair
as he came closer to pull the slip
from my hand, push the thumb from my mouth.
All of Boston's winter rushed the open window,

and he flung the satin slip—in a flutter
it dimmed like a child's ghost
with all that darkness beneath. I saw

the moves of a soldier, his hands
finishing at the window,
seven floors up in the dark.

Airplane Conversation
with an Engineer
Who Designed Ammunition

M A R Y   A N N   W A T E R S

He seemed the right one to ask.
After dessert, the initial exchange,
I said, cluster bombs, how

do they work.
Efficiently, he said, using his hands
to model a unit attached to the wing

of a plane. The pilot drops one
or six at a time. Or twelve,
they're designed not to kill,

and he stopped.
I remembered reports from Sidon
and spoke of the casualties there.

He said, I can't think of that.
As the plane touched down he confided
this night was his child's graduation

and he would miss the event.
She's been to the beauty parlor, he said,
her dress is cotton batiste.

Clearly, he saw himself with the Pentax,
his daughter posed this way and that.
Perhaps he imagined her

squinting just after the flash,
just before she said, ''That's enough, Daddy,''
though he would have taken more.

The Food Pickers of Saigon

WALTER McDONALD

Rubbish like compost heaps burned every hour
of my days and nights at Tan Son Nhut.
Ragpickers scoured the edges of our junk,
risking the flames, bent over,
searching for food. A ton of tin cans

piled up each month, sharp edged, unlabeled.
Those tiny anonymous people could stick
their hands inside and claw out whatever
remained, scooping it into jars, into their
mouths. No one went hungry. At a distance,

the dump was like a coal mine fire burning
out of control, or Moses' holy bush
which was not consumed. Watching them labor
in the field north of my barracks, trying
to think of something good to write my wife,

I often thought of bears in Yellowstone
our first good summer in a tent. I wrote
about the bears, helping us both focus
on how they waddled to the road and begged,
and came some nights into the campground

so long ago and took all food they found.
We sat helplessly naive outside our tent
and watched them, and one night rolled
inside laughing when one great bear
turned and shoulder-swayed his way toward us.

Through the zipped mosquito netting
we watched him watching us. Slack-jawed,
he seemed to grin, to thank us for all
he was about to receive from our table.
We thought how lovely, how much fun

to be this close to danger. No campers
had died in that Disneyland national park
for years. Now, when my children
eat their meat and bread and leave
good broccoli or green beans

on their plates, I call them back
and growl, I can't help it. It's like hearing
my father's voice again. I never tell them
why they have to eat it. I never say
they're like two beautiful children

I found staring at me one night
through the screen of my window,
at Tan Son Nhut, bone-faced. Or that
when I crawled out of my stifling monsoon
dream to feed them, they were gone.

The Penance

LEONARD NATHAN

This is the penance: a recurring dream,
This child running down the road, its mouth
A hole filled up with blackness, its little wings
Two flares of napalm and it runs toward you.

You can't yet hear its scream but know it's screaming,
Know if it can reach you, it will try to
Hug you and that napalm is contagious,
A deadly foreign plague for darker people.

Nothing can save you—voting, letters, marches—
So you close your eyes. A hundred years
It seems to take, the child getting nearer,
Bigger, maybe not so scared as furious.

Now you hear its scream—a supersonic
Jet-like whine that peels your skin off patch
By patch, and then the face is in your face,
Close as a lover's, eyes as bleak as bullets.

Then black-out till you wake forgetting all,
Forgetting him who felt the burning arms
Around him, but who can't, it seems, save any
Thing that matters though he knows what matters.

So this is the penance: a recurring dream
That you're awake and doing good, loving
The children, saving for their education
And your own retirement—till you close your eyes.

Vietnam War Memorial

ROBERT MORGAN

What we see first seems a shadow
or a retaining wall in the park,
like half a giant pool or half
an exposed foundation. The names
start a few to the column at
the shallow ends and grow panel
by deeper panel as though month
by month to the point of opposing
planes. From that pit you can't see much
official Washington, just sky
and trees and names and people on
the Mall and the Capitol like
a fancy urn. For this is a wedge
into the earth, a ramp of names
driven into the nation's green,
a black mirror of names many
as the text of a book published
in stone, beginning almost
imperceptibly in the lawn
on one side and growing on black
pages bigger than any reader
(as you look for your own name in
each chapter) and then thin away
like a ledger into turf again,
with no beginning, no end. As though
the black wall uncovered here a few
rods for sunlight and recognition
runs on and on through the ground in
both directions, with all our names
on the hidden panels, while
these names shine in the open noon.

Saying Farewell, He Shows Me His Vietnam Poems

RAY GONZALEZ

Student of mine, with the worn face,
you reveal the truth on the last day,
show me how many you killed before
you put down your first words,
this surprise of experience
you concealed quite well,
fleeing images of gunships and napalm
finally exploding on the page,
your quiet search for the better poem
ambushed by the VC in your sleep,
your stanzas about love and family torn
by recurring squawks of the radio man.

Student of words, lost in the jungle,
you know how to say good-bye,
how to brand the poem into the brain
like the Vietnamese child running
with her arms on fire,
your poem listing how often
you had to do it,
how many days you had left in-country,
how long it has taken to learn
how to write about it,
how to breathe amidst the napalm,
when to sing with joy,
when to whisper the other truth
that it is time to say farewell
to things that keep you
tied to the poem.

The Challenge

G E O F   H E W I T T

So what kind of poetry you write?
he finally asked after smoking in silence
half the cigarette he'd borrowed.
Waiting for my flowers and moons he thought up
the one he wrote about a dying white
horse in Vietnam, how the Montagnards
wouldn't let the Tennessee GIs put it out
of its misery and they were going crazy
seeing it—guts blown out—suffer.
This was what he brought home
and after hearing my credentials told me:
that if he could write it, he would.
Was I serious enough? Did I care?
Would I just tack on a fourteenth line to make it a sonnet?

the hard way

S H E R Y L   L .   N E L M S

he was the lesson
for the other Cambodian prisoners

without a word

hands and feet
roped tight

he was dropped over the side
into a huge
copper
pit

screaming and sizzling
as skin touched
mortifying metal

his screams fading
to moans
as he cooked

the popping of fat frying
finally fading to
charred black

that cinder frame

pushing the others back
to their hard
labor

In San Salvador (I)

GRACE PALEY

Come   look   they said
here are the photograph albums
these are our children

We are called The Mothers of the Disappeared
we are also the mothers of those who were seen once more
and then photographed   sometimes parts of them
could not be found

a breast   an eye   an arm is missing
sometimes a whole stomach
that is why we are called   The Mothers
of the Disappeared   although we have these large
heavy photograph albums full of beautiful
torn faces

Aftermath

J U N E   J O R D A N

Morning sun heats up the young beech tree
leaves and almost lights them into fireflies

I wish I could dig up the earth to plant apples
pears or peaches on a lazy dandelion lawn

I am tired from this digging up of human bodies
no one loved enough to save from death

Poem Ending with an Old Cliché

P A U L   Z I M M E R

"Dr. Caldwell wants to trace the other participants in the
exercise, the purpose of which was to test soldiers' reactions
to a nuclear blast. . . . 'There have been some erroneous
accounts as to the amount of radiation those men were
exposed to.' " —*Parade*, June 19, 1977

Last week my old cat fell to the worms;
I watched the clouds come down into his eyes,
The final twitch and turn of his muscles
Like the pinnae of a clipped fern,

Constricting in sadness, clutching in to ease
The final cravings, then the fearful resignation.
Seeing this, I can say the old cliché now,
Knowing at long last what it means:
Life is precious. It is all we have.

How was I to know through all my long
And short years that two decades beyond
The flash and ram of those explosions,
The vaporized towers and mangled animals,
Caved-in trenches and awesome dawn clouds,
I might finally bear secrets?

In whatever dimness and despair,
In the midst of terrible exchanges,
From down on my knees in fear
Of early death, senility or loss;
Even in happiness it cannot be forgotten.
I will say it again. It has become the truth:
Life is precious.

Family Portrait 1933

PETER ORESICK

In the center my grandfather sits
a patriarch, a boy on his knee
and progeny surrounding. His face says
this is my contribution, but the lips wanting
reassurance. My grandmother is a trunk
of a woman three children wide,
her face stern and unfathomable.

While they are stiff and attentive,
I would like to speak.
Father, I'd say, you are twenty
now, but will lease your body out
to machines like the man did
on whose shoulder you rest your hand.
And after forty years you'll say
"I'm just an old man smoking cigarettes
in the cellar, fixing radios."
Uncles, aunts, I cannot keep track
of you. **Live.**
Grandfather, grandmother, don't worry.
I'll be born in twenty-two years
and grow strong and bury you.
Uncle Mike, old mole,
you will bury yourself
in the anthracite fields of Pennsylvania.
Please resume now. Come unfrozen,
quickly; do what you must do.

Family

GRACE PALEY

My father was brilliant   embarrassed   funny   handsome
my mother was plain   serious   principled   kind
my grandmother was intelligent   lonesome for her
                    other life   her dead children   silent
my aunt was beautiful   bitter   angry   loving

I fell among these adjectives in earliest childhood
and was nearly buried with opportunity
some of them stuck to me   others
finding me American and smooth slipped away

Four Roses

SUSAN WOOD

Outside my door four roses
languish in the late spring sun. They don't
smell of failure yet, though he did, who hid
Four Roses in a cardboard suitcase. In memory
they call my uncle "Rabbit" because he runs
like that. Red-faced, he crouches
in the infield, short, and makes the dive
and throws to first. One out. I'm six
and sitting in the bleachers the summer
Eisenhower thought to save the world again, proud
to be his niece. The Fort Worth Cats are all the sport
there is. My father says I have it wrong.
By 1952 the whiskey stopped him, he hadn't played
in years, just coached, and that not much.
But I'd rather believe him home
and safe than think of the day my father,
out with his boss, saw a bum weaving

down a city street, a bottle of Four Roses
in his hand. Something in his walk gave him away.
My father turned back to the road, drove on
and on. The last time I saw my uncle he stooped
and shuffled when he walked, left a pile
of crumbs around his plate. It's an old story.
Next week I'll be forty and he'll be dead
five months who raised Four Roses to his lips
and drank. And what is memory
if not the glare of a sun-drenched field
where an almost Texas Leaguer pops up
and up and Rabbit opens his glove
to catch it, one hand, and end the game?

(C.W.M., 1910–1985)

The Most Haunted

R O B E R T   L O U T H A N

for my sister

I'm sorry you were born
on October 31, sorry
if I paid more attention that day
to Halloween than to you
each year when we were young.

But maybe you imagined all the children
excited on the streets that night,
dressed in their deadly little costumes,
were celebrating your birthday.

The night you were born,
a month after our father died,
the scariest skeleton
was the one in his grave,
and our house the most haunted.

For a Sister Not Yet Dead

ELLIOT FRIED

My nephew told me—she had taken
pills and wine but instead of slipping
into the soft haze of sleep, she floated
outside to the drive, slumped into the car, gunned it,
and smashed into the metal garage door.
Her daughters got her out, but she couldn't walk,
just staggered, lurched, and fell
onto the stunted grass. Her shallow breathing
slowed, then stopped. They screamed and pounded
on her breasts. The paramedics came
and took her to a hospital. When she
finally woke, she asked, "Am I still
alive?"
        In 1953, when I was nine,
I remember she locked herself inside
the bathroom, threatened razor blades.
The firemen were called—they broke the door
and dragged her out. Behind a chair, I watched.
I couldn't understand, but that was then.
Again and yet again she made the choice—
enough—enough for here, for now . . .
but things went wrong. The blood wouldn't leak,
the heart wouldn't stop, and so she asked
in a strange room, "Am I still alive?"
                    Perhaps
next time, my sister. Perhaps next time. It's
only peace. I know now that
the seasons in the gray unruly night
all vindicate the slash of blade, the pill,
the gas left on, the gun. The journey's much
too long. The air, a vice grip, clutches you
too tight. Your fingers twitch in the dark wind
and death, a bright red ball you toss lightly

above your head, skitters from your fingertips,
so soft you can almost feel. The oily
residue of men and children gone, the daily
Rubik's Cube—why try to mesh the sullen days,
the bloated afternoons, when nothing ever happens
but the night?

A pill, a water glass, a razor blade,
all tickets to a place where you just are
and everything around you finally stops.

anorexia neurosis

SHERYL L. NELMS

sucking ice cubes
instead of eating

she reminds me of that fish

the Egyptian mouthbreeder
lips locked
coddling
those
eggs

while her body evaporates

fat reservoirs gone
toothpick ribs
prick
out
against caved-in skin

hovering in a shadowed corner

she savors
her total dedication

Winter Stars

L A R R Y   L E V I S

My father once broke a man's hand
Over the exhaust pipe of a John Deere tractor. The man,
Rubén Vásquez, wanted to kill his own father
With a sharpened fruit knife, & he held
The curved tip of it, lightly, between his first
Two fingers, so it could slash
Horizontally, & with surprising grace,
Across a throat. It was like a glinting beak in a hand,
And, for a moment, the light held still
On those vines. When it was over,
My father simply went in & ate lunch, & then, as always,
Lay alone in the dark, listening to music.
He never mentioned it.

I never understood how anyone could risk his life,
Then listen to Vivaldi.

Sometimes, I go out into this yard at night,
And stare through the wet branches of an oak
In winter, & realize I am looking at the stars
Again. A thin haze of them, shining
And persisting.

It used to make me feel lighter, looking up at them.
In California, that light was closer.
In a California no one will ever see again,

My father is beginning to die. Something
inside him is slowly taking back
Every word it ever gave him.
Now, if we try to talk, I watch my father
Search for a lost syllable as if it might
Solve everything, & though he can't remember, now,
The word for it, he is ashamed. . . .
If you can think of the mind as a place continually
Visited, a whole city placed behind
The eyes, & shining, I can imagine, now, its end—
As when the lights go off, one by one,
In a hotel at night, until at last
All of the travelers will be asleep, or until
Even the thin glow from the lobby is a kind
Of sleep; & while the woman behind the desk
Is applying more lacquer to her nails,
You can almost believe that the elevator,
As it ascends, must open upon starlight.

I stand out on the street, & do not go in.
That was our agreement, at my birth.

And for years I believed
That what went unsaid between us became empty,
And pure, like starlight, & that it persisted.

I got it all wrong.
I wound up believing in words the way a scientist
Believes in carbon, after death.

Tonight, I'm talking to you, Father, although
It is quiet here in the Midwest, where a small wind,
The size of a wrist, wakes the cold again—
Which may be all that's left of you & me.

When I left home at seventeen, I left for good.

That pale haze of stars goes on & on,
Like laughter that has found a final, silent shape
On a black sky. It means everything
It cannot say. Look, it's empty out there, & cold.
Cold enough to reconcile
Even a father, even a son.

The Absent Father

LEE SHARKEY

Perhaps a wish, perhaps a memory
                of rocking in your arms.

Reaching up to you
                expecting to be lifted to the sky.

Riding piggyback. Playing Trust Me:
standing straight and falling back and you would catch—
                no, that was Uncle Dan.

Hiking down a grassy slope, across a dusty field
to a huge yellow tent, roped and staked,
and inside: girls in pink
swivel on circling elephants, trapeze families
swing from the roof, wide-mouthed clowns
pratfall, lunge at us in the front row—
                me and Uncle Jerry.

Summer days at the ocean, I learn the math
of waves, the pulse of tide
                with Mother.

With you, what voyage?
What event or conversation, you and I?
What skill, what lore?

Not learning to ride a bike
or skate or read or write
or dance or sing in any language
or play a finger game or pray—

For a moment, you put down your paper,
let me kiss your cheek good night.
But nothing! nothing
to remember I learned to live
to love us by.

Jack's Flashlight

CHASE TWICHELL

Three years old, my nephew
strafes the dark pines
from the porch with his flashlight.
His father has gone away,
leaving a boat carved from kindling.
Late in August, this far north,
the ground is already cold.
Smoke, pine, and recent rain
will mark this night
and drag it back to him.
I remember when my father
changed the way he loved me.
With my hands over my ears
I watched his power saw
whiten the barn door
with drifts of sawdust,
sweet burn-smell persisting.
Jack hunches in the chill
intersection of here and now,
and carves at the trees with
the bleaching beam of abandonment.

My Mother,
If She Had Won Free Dance Lessons

C O R N E L I U S   E A D Y

Would she have been a person
With a completely different outlook on life?
There are times when I visit
And find her settled on a chair
In our dilapidated house,
The neighborhood crazy lady
Doing what the neighborhood crazy lady is
        supposed to do,
Which is absolutely nothing

And I wonder as we talk our sympathetic talk,
Abandoned in easy dialogue,
I, the son of the crazy lady,
Who crosses easily into her point of view
As if yawning
Or taking off an overcoat.
Each time I visit
I walk back into our lives

And I wonder, like any child who wakes up one day
        to find themselves
Abandoned in a world larger than their
        bad dreams,
I wonder as I see my mother sitting there,
Landed to the right-hand window in the living room,
Pausing from time to time in the endless loop
        of our dialogue
To peek for rascals through the
Venetian blinds,

I wonder a small thought.
I walk back into our lives.

Given the opportunity,
How would she have danced?
Would it have been as easily
As we talk to each other now,
The crazy lady
And the crazy lady's son,
As if we were old friends from opposite coasts
Picking up the thread of a long conversation,

Or two ballroom dancers
Who only know
One step?

What would have changed
If the phone had rung like a suitor,
If the invitation had arrived in the mail
Like Jesus, extending a hand?

Nursing Home

SAM CORNISH

in Brookline
in Newton
where the blacks are poor
and the bombs
fall in other countries
it is polite
to hide your mother
when she is old and walking
after midnight
in a thin nightgown

Moving My Grandfather

JIM DANIELS

He wouldn't move
after fifty years in the same house.
He put a burglar alarm sign on his door
a chewed-up shoe in his yard
a baseball bat by the door
though he had no alarm, dog, strength.

He didn't carry a wallet.
Pinned money to his shirt
but had no sign for that.
He got jumped often
for change not worth
kicking an old man's ass for.

Last time they cracked his skull
blood in his white hair.
He came out of the hospital
lobotomized by fear
sitting in his front room
listening to the street.

We packed up his belongings
three broken tvs
a stringless harp from the burned-out
church across the street.
My father cried its music
up and down the stairs.

We loaded up fast, in daylight
one truckload. No one could figure out
how to free the rocking chair
chained to the porch
so we left it
creaking in the heavy air.

Eastern Standard

D A V I D   H U D D L E

Riled by Daylight
Savings, Grandmama
Huddle kept her
clocks unchanged.
Summers she was off
an hour and irked
at the Democrats
responsible
for inflation,
integration,
and now this
further indignity.

Disoriented
her last years
in a nursing home,
she shrank
until she became
an old-lady doll,
restrained in bed
and railing
to the bare,
urine-scented
room about bad food,
bad manners,
and the Kennedys.

At ninety-nine
she finally died.
I'm forty-seven.
Yesterday I stole
an hour
from a clock of hers
that has come down

to me. This morning
when I checked
my watch
against the light
outside the window,
my grandmother
spoke sharply:
"What time
is it, sonny?
And don't you
lie to me!"

His Grandmother Talks about God

PAUL RUFFIN

"I have come, in recent years,
to think different about God,"
she said to the lean young men
who called, dressed in dark suits,
each with a Bible on his knee.
"I'm not so sure, as I once was."
Neither of them said a word.
"Ah, He once was so soft and good,
like some feathered thing to lie
down on and rest, in those days
before I had lived long and hard
enough and suffered enough to learn."
They looked at each other, then away.
Their fingers made crosses on the Bibles.
"He is what we make Him, want Him to be.
When we are young, He is tender
with our years, warm, and exceeding
bright with the wings we dream Him."

They nodded and watched her face.
"And when we are old and hard and
perhaps not so very good, He loses
what we lost and becomes, like us,
fierce and dark and wingless,
waiting for the night to come."

Heaven for Railroad Men

DAVID   WOJAHN

You're still a young man,
he says, not to his son,
it's his bitterness he's
talking to and
at the restaurant
he orders a fourth round
before dinner.
With Mother wiping
her glasses at the table,

I help him from his chair
to the john. He pees slowly,
fingers like hams
on his fly, a complex
test of logic
for a man this drunk.
I'm splashing cold water in his face

and he tells me he's dying,
Don't say a thing to your mother,
and please, Dave,
don't ever remember me like this.

I remember how you said you
needed to ride
the baggage cars forever,
passing prairie towns
where silos squat like
pepper shakers on dry earth.
I want to be six again
and sway with you
down the sagging rails
to Minot, Winnipeg, and beyond,
your mailsacks piled
like foothills of the Rockies.

You're unloading your government Colt,
unzipping your suitcase
for Canadian inspectors.
Father, when I touched you
I was trembling.

Heaven for railroad men
begins with a collapsed trestle.
The engine goes steaming
off into nothing.
There are no rails to hold you.
You're singing country-western
at the top of your lungs.
You go flying forever,
the door pulled open,
mailsacks scattered
into space like seed.

To My Sons on Father's Day

ROBERT A. FINK

You would have liked me
younger, careless,
my hair wild
like I'd just swung off a Harley.
I didn't talk much then,
knew nothing interesting but the weekend.
Everybody died at thirty.

Could you believe
I had this rolled and pleated Ford
and a girl from Waxahachie?
How about turning twenty-one on the coast
walking the Santa Monica waves,
dancing the Monkey with a topless waitress?

I understand.
You've only known me after Nam,
marriage vows
I raised my hand
and swore to honor.

What happened was
I didn't die
and learned to read headlines.

Thank you for the tie
and after shave lotion.
The tee shirt with the cartoon penguin,
top hat apologetic in his hand.

Eye of the Beholder

MARK VINZ

for Sarah

"I've often wondered what it would be like to be beautiful.
I've never had the problem." —Paul Zimmer

We're always reminded, aren't we—
on every screen, on every page
we turn. Perhaps somehow we too
might find a way to measure up,
the secret of each serene gaze . . .

Today we go shopping, my fine
tall daughter and I—who looms
above the others in the store
that pause in aisles to gape
at what they think they see.

She smiles and looks at me
as if to say it doesn't matter,
even if we both know
there are times and ways it does.
But what we also know is this:

Beautiful is understanding what you
cannot ask from those who stare—
more than their eyes, more than ours.
And beautiful is finally judged
by all the reasons that you're missed.

Tristem

D O R I A N N E   L A U X

Tonight, when I peeled my uniform to the floor,
coins and bills fell from my pockets
like confetti and lead; sharp clinks
that trapped me in the anger of this afternoon
when Tristem, skating through the kitchen,
knocked into the table breaking the fruit bowl.
Rind everywhere and late for work
I glared up at her from my knees.
Bawling with apology
she had only wanted forgiveness.
But I had clenched my teeth and gnawed on dreams
of freedom, wanting to start up fresh and alone
in an empty house.

Curled up in a wedge of moonlight my only child
sleeps beneath the open window.
In a high corner of her room a dragonfly kite
hovers at the end of a string, dipping
now and then in the breeze.
A wooden airplane, smaller than my fist
on the booklined valance above her bed.
Her crown of hay hair stuffed into the pillow;
behind her lips, a missing tooth.
Sitting in the dark among her small things
I'm struck by how soundly she sleeps;
by how the moon has climbed up my legs
unfolding itself like a handkerchief on my lap;
watching the kite flutter and drift,
wanting only forgiveness,
wanting only to be in this room.

Family

DEL MARIE ROGERS

I want to bring back my grandfather, Richard Thomas,
tamping pipe tobacco with a big, worn thumb,
his battle-worn tomcat Pixie, nobody else's lap-cat,
dozing on his knees. Sun on the radio.
Or standing in the dim tool shed, under the apricot.
Getting up at five in the morning
to make smelly bait, to boil coffee.

I'm not thinking only of him.
I am thinking of myself,
I want the sun through branches heavy with apricots,
so slow there is no word for time.
Or the grape arbor whose intricate knots
wrapped the back screened porch.
I slept in a tangle of leaves.

Uncle Dick, they called him, in Chickasha, Oklahoma.
He was once mayor of a small town,
knew how it felt to lose everything—
property, money in the Great Depression.
His first wife, Pearl Grey, part Chickasaw,
left their baby, Toy, behind,
ran away to another life.

I'll search for words or my children won't know
he endured the worst of it,
stood quiet and steady.
They've never seen anything like that:
long winters of staying alive.
What will my children say about me?
I was the one who wrote this down.

Delicate

MATTHEW GRAHAM

My friend's father's last word was *unbelievable*,
A word my friend attributes not to
His father's view of death, but to
The passing of time—of how unbelievably fast
It all goes. And my friend realizes this,
Now all the more, as his children begin to pass him by.
And he tells me this as I'm about to visit
My own father, so much younger than I am now
When he had me—this father who seems now
To seek my company after such a long absence,
Though that absence was probably all mine.
All this as my wife and I try to conceive
Our own child—something we've both waited too long,
To become the right people, to be able to take on.
We pass sometimes in the hall or on the stairs
Of this rented house that has seen so many pass,
And I wonder who she is, this woman I've known
Like no one else. Just this morning from the window I saw
That the first shock of forsythia was gone. Unbelievable,
How something so delicate can move so fast.

Acknowledgments

While every effort has been made to secure permission, it has in a few cases proved impossible to trace the author or author's executor. Permission to reprint poems is gratefully acknowledged to the following:

ADASTRA PRESS, for "Anna Marie" from *Other Lives* by Peter Oresick, copyright © 1985 by Peter Oresick, reprinted by permission of the publisher.

THE ANTIOCH REVIEW, for "Bones in an African Cave" by Peter Meinke, copyright © 1966 by The Antioch Review, Inc.

ANTLER, for "Raising My Hand" from *Last Words*, copyright © 1986 by Antler.

APPALACHIAN JOURNAL, for "Stripped" by George Ella Lyon (originally appeared in *Appalachian Journal*, Volume 8, Number 3, Spring 1981), copyright © 1981 by *Appalachian Journal*.

GRACE BAUER, for "The Visiting Paleontologist Feels Her Thigh" from *South Dakota Review*.

CARLETON COLLEGE, for "Help Is on the Way" (has appeared in *The Carleton Miscellany*, Volume XI, Number 1, Winter 1970) by Herbert Scott, copyright © 1969 by Carleton College.

HENRY CARLILE, for "Conscientious Objector" from *Tar River Poetry* (also to be published in *Rain*, Carnegie Mellon University Press, 1993) by Henry Carlile, copyright © 1992 by *Tar River Poetry*, East Carolina University.

CARNEGIE MELLON UNIVERSITY PRESS, for "Live Studio Wrestling" from *The Lady from the Dark Green Hills* by Jim Hall, copyright © 1977 by Jim Hall, and for "White Trash" from *False Statements* by Jim Hall, copyright © 1986 by Jim Hall, both poems reprinted by permission of the publisher.

CINTO PUNTOS PRESS, for "The Old Man & His Calf" from *Lion's Gate* by Keith Wilson, reprinted by permission of the author.

MARY CLARK, for "Talking Long Distance after One A.M."

CLARKE IRWIN, LTD., for "He Attempts to Love His Neighbors" from *I Might Not Tell Everybody This* by Alden Nowlan, copyright © 1983 by Clarke Irwin, Ltd., copyright © 1982 by Alden Nowlan.

VIC COCCIMIGLIO, for "House Keys."

CONFLUENCE PRESS, INC., for "Airplane Conversation with an Engineer Who Designed Ammunition" from *The Exact Place* by Mary Ann Waters, copyright © 1987 by Confluence Press, Inc., and Mary Ann Waters.

COPPER BEECH PRESS, for "To an Estranged Wife" from *The Dream of a Moral Life* by Gary Young, copyright © 1990 by Gary Young.

CORONA PUBLISHING COMPANY, for "Family" and "I Have Some Questions about Life on Earth" from *Close to Ground* (1991) by Del Marie Rogers.

LEO DANGEL, for "Restoring the Ecology" from *Hogs and Personals* (Spoon River Poetry Press), copyright © 1992 by Leo Dangel, and for "The Belt Buckle" and "How to Take a Walk" from *Old Man Brunner Country* (Spoon River Poetry Press), copyright © 1987 by Leo Dangel.

BILL DODD, for "Hunting on the Homefront" (originally published in *Rio Grande Review*, Volume 6, Number 2, Spring 1987), copyright © 1987 by Bill Dodd.

DAVID ALLAN EVANS, for "Tom Lonehill (1940–1956)" from *Poetry Now*, copyright © 1992 by David Allan Evans.

DAVID EVANS, JR., for "Lonely Games" and "Newlyweds," copyright © 1992 by David Evans, Jr.

EDWARD FIELD, for "The Two Orders of Love" from *A Full Heart* (1977), reprinted by permission of the author.

ROBERT A. FINK, for "To My Sons on Father's Day" and "Why Is It," copyright © 1992 by Robert A. Fink.

RALPH FLETCHER, for "Waiting for the Splash" from *Water Planet*, copyright © 1992 by Ralph Fletcher.

KATHERINE SONIAT, for "War" from *Poet Lore*, copyright © 1992 by Katherine Soniat.

SPOON RIVER POETRY PRESS, for "No Woman Is Ever Prepared" by Deborah Bosley.

JAMES STRECKER, for "Ineffable Beauty."

TALKING STONE PRESS, for "Gossip" and "Leaving" from *A Living Anytime* by Judith W. Steinbergh, copyright © 1988 by Judith W. Steinbergh.

THUNDER'S MOUTH PRESS, for "Aftermath" from *Naming Our Destiny* by June Jordan, copyright © 1989 by June Jordan, reprinted by permission of the publisher.

TILBURY HOUSE, PUBLISHERS, for "Family" and "In San Salvador (I)" from *New and Collected Poems* by Grace Paley, copyright © 1992 by Grace Paley, reprinted by permission of the publisher.

RODNEY TORRESON, for "Harold Iverson, Teacher" and "Matthew Schnell" from *The Hiram Poetry Review*, copyright © 1992 by Rodney Torreson.

ANN TOWNSEND, for "Play," copyright © 1992 by Ann Townsend; and for "Purple Loosestrife" from *New Virginia Review*, copyright © 1991 by Ann Townsend.

UNICORN PRESS, INC., for "Nursing Home" from *Songs of Jubilee* by Sam Cornish.

UNIVERSITY OF ARKANSAS PRESS, for "Patriotics" from *Sweet Home, Saturday Night* by David Baker, copyright © 1991 by David Baker.

UNIVERSITY OF ILLINOIS PRESS, for "When Bosses Sank Steel Islands" (originally published in *Palladium*) by Alice Fulton; and for "For Poppa, Asleep in the Smithtown Madhouse" (originally published in *Waiting for Poppa at the Smithtown Diner*) by Peter Serchuk.

THE UNIVERSITY OF MASSACHUSETTS PRESS, for "The Food Pickers of Saigon" and "The Rodeo Fool" from *After the Noise of Saigon* by Walter McDonald, copyright © 1988 by Walter McDonald.

WEST END PRESS, for "Family Portrait 1933" from *Definitions* by Peter Oresick, copyright © 1990 by Peter Oresick.

KEITH WILSON, for "The Old Man & His Calf" from *Lion's Gate* (Cinto Puntos Press) by Keith Wilson, reprinted by permission of the author.

WRITERS AND READERS PUBLISHING, INC., for "wounds #13" by Safiya Henderson-Holmes.

YALE UNIVERSITY PRESS, for "Heaven for Railroad Men" from *Icehouse Lights* (1982) by David Wojahn.

GARY YOUNG, for "Out of the Mines" from *Hands* (1979), copyright © 1979 by Gary Young.

REE YOUNG, for "When Leland Left Elma" from *Spoon River Quarterly*, copyright © 1992 by Ree Young.

PAUL ZIMMER, for "Poem Ending with an Old Cliché," copyright © 1981 by Paul Zimmer.

Index of First Lines

Any cow with half a brain could see   *43*

at the half-price book table in the mall,   *91*

August, another year and the same   *52*

Because we were 18 and still wonderful in our bodies,   *89*

Bones in an African cave   *81*

Come   look   they said   *104*

Convolvulus it's called as well, or ill,   *16*

Dear Ann, I think I am losing my husband.   *60*

deceive. Where is there school   *69*

Elma called it witchcraft. I say   *55*

Everyone knows what the shortest distance   *18*

Everything has become a museum.   *33*

First of all,   *59*

He lived alone. Had a kitten but it died.   *14*

He seemed the right one to ask.   *97*

he was the lesson   *103*

He wouldn't move   *118*

Home, he is known   *62*

Hoping he'll get run over, go off   *48*

I close my eyes   *53*

I confess all creatures I have killed: *49*

I found him stumbling about when the mother   *47*

"I have come, in recent years,   *120*

I have never signed   *12*

I have no lips, no nose.   *83*

I have to watch my wife.   *66*

I live in the Nez Perce country   *95*

I want to bring back my grandfather, Richard Thomas,   *126*

I want to play tough, beating my brother   *20*

I was humming "Mist on the Mountain"   *7*

I'm sorry you were born   *109*

I've been fighting   *32*

If I should be told,   *37*

In an old house   *86*

in Brookline   *117*

In high school he quit them all: *93*

In the center my grandfather sits   *107*
In the lonely games   *19*
in the North Sea, I was issued this survival   *74*
Is diabetes catching, he asks,   *39*
It wasn't riding the bus across town, eyeing my feet   *21*
Last night   *52*
Last week my old cat fell to the worms;   *105*
Late at night when I walk home   *82*
Laying off, they're laying off   *77*
Leveling his pole like some quixotic lance,   *29*
Mel Brown was teaching us   *26*
Morning sun heats up the young beech tree   *105*
My father once broke a man's hand   *112*
My father remembers a nurse   *8*
My father was brilliant   embarrassed   funny   handsome   *108*
My friend's father's last word was *unbelievable,*   *127*
My mother said he was real,   *96*
My neighbors do not wish to be loved.   *53*
My nephew told me—she had taken   *110*
None of us were winners, like   *23*
Nothing's too good for the women   *88*
Now it's Styrofoam pellets   *9*
On the telephone, breaking up   *57*
One of the first things we learn in school is   *1*
Opposed to crewcuts and buddies,   *30*
Our parakeet escaped from the house on the highest day   *46*
Outside my door four roses   *108*
Perhaps a wish, perhaps a memory   *114*
Remember how the door in our first apartment always stuck?   *56*
Riled by Daylight   *119*
Rubbish like compost heaps burned every hour   *98*
She has flowers   *13*
She has missed Mass again.   *68*
She was a mother you could count on. She was like the sun   *69*
she was there, on her   *82*
Silver Lake has changed into a milky,   *24*
Since you died I try to pull you back   *34*
So what kind of poetry you write?   *103*
Student of mine, with the worn face,   *102*
sucking ice cubes   *111*

Suppose some peddler offered   *79*

. . . that he'll never sell, though   *43*

The day after her mother died   *35*

The great wall is crumbling   *87*

The Murfreesboro Mauler peels   *22*

The sun glints on his weapon   *92*

There's no use putting it off, Audrey,   *65*

This is farming country.   *46*

This is the penance: a recurring dream,   *100*

This one's gone to straw   I cannot say   *15*

Three shifts of weaving and cutting,   *76*

Three years old, my nephew   *115*

Through dust deepened by others   *93*

To create   *50*

Tonight, when I peeled my uniform to the floor,   *125*

Two Indians draped in buffalo robes   *10*

Under clouds, I walk through lupine,   *63*

understand why   *45*

Walter always took   *65*

was too good to be true, in all its definitions.   *17*

We badgered him for days on the playground   *83*

We burn the coal in our lungs   *75*

We did not know the first thing about   *36*

We have every right to hate them, he said,   *58*

We hummed sad country songs all summer,   *27*

We're always reminded, aren't we—   *124*

What we see first seems a shadow   *101*

When our milk goats and their kids cavorted   *88*

When they knew you were sick   *41*

Where are they, for Christ's sake,   *25*

whose stamp albums saved us   *84*

Why did the trees stop casting   *5*

Would she have been a person   *116*

Yesterday a little girl got slapped to death by her daddy,   *73*

You still wake trembling   *86*

You would have liked me   *123*

You're still a young man,   121

Index of Authors and Titles

Absent Father, The   *114*

After Quarreling   *63*

Aftermath   *105*

Airplane Conversation with an Engineer Who Designed Ammunition   *97*

Anna Marie   *68*

anorexia neurosis   *111*

Antler   *1*

Appearances   *69*

Baker, David   *73*

Barker, Wendy   *39*

Bauer, Grace   *62*

Belt Buckle, The   *65*

Best Dance Hall in Iuka, Mississippi, The   *88*

Black Thumb, The   *14*

Blue Collar   *76*

Bones in an African Cave   *81*

Bosley, Deborah   *35*

Buckley, Christopher   *89*

Burnt Child, The   *83*

Burying   *47*

Carlile, Henry   *93*

Challenge   *29*

Challenge, The   *103*

Clark, Mary   *57*

Coach Goes down the Hall Wondering Where All the Men Went   *25*

Coccimiglio, Vic   *82*

Confession, Curse and Prayer   *49*

Conscientious Objector   *93*

Cornish, Sam   *117*

Dangel, Leo   *13, 46, 65*

Daniels, Jim   *77, 118*

Delicate   *127*

Distance   *18*

Dodd, Bill   *95*

Eady, Cornelius   *116*

Eastern Standard   *119*

Enticing Lane, The   *37*

Evans, David Allan   *30*

Evans, David, Jr.   *19, 66*

Even When   *53*

Eye of the Beholder   *124*

Failures of Pacifism, The   *88*

Family (Grace Paley)   *108*

Family (Del Marie Rogers)   *126*

Family Portrait 1933   *107*

Field, Edward   *58*

Fink, Robert A.   *91, 123*

Flames   *83*

Fletcher, Ralph   *52*

Food Pickers of Saigon, The   *98*

For a Sister Not Yet Dead   *110*

For Generations   *10*

For Poppa, Asleep in the Smithtown Madhouse   *41*

Four Roses   *108*

Fried, Elliot   *110*

Fulton, Alice   *74*

Gildner, Gary   *21*

Gone Astray: Little Miss Muffet   *59*

Gonzalez, Ray   *102*

Gossip   *69*

Graham, Matthew   *127*

Hall, Jim   *9, 22*

hard way, the   *103*

Harold Iverson, Teacher   *84*

Hazo, Samuel   *29*

He Attempts to Love His Neighbors   *53*

Heaven for Railroad Men   *121*

Help Is on the Way   *60*

Hemp, Christine   *34, 53*

Henderson-Holmes, Safiya   *82*

Hewitt, Christopher   *37*

Hewitt, Geof   *23, 103*

Hey, Phil   *69*

His Grandmother Talks about God   *120*

Holden, Jonathan   *24, 26*

House Keys   *82*

How to Take a Walk   *46*

Huddle, David   *119*

Hunting on the Homefront   95

I Have Some Questions about Life on Earth   5

I Hear the River Call My Name   32

i'll never   45

Ice Hockey   24

Iddings, Kathleen   *43, 86*

Identifying Things   39

In San Salvador (I)   104

Ineffable Beauty   50

Jack's Flashlight   115

James, David   *59*

Johnson, Thomas   *88*

Jordan, June   *105*

Joyce, Jane Wilson   *86*

Karate   26

Killing the Dog   48

Koertge, Ronald   *14*

LaBombard, Joan   *92*

Laux, Dorianne   *125*

Leaving   46

Letting the Plants Die   15

Levis, Larry   *112*

Live Studio Wrestling   22

Lonely Games   19

Louthan, Robert   *109*

Lyon, George Ella   *7*

Market Economy, The   79

married 3 months   65

Matthew Schnell   93

McDonald, Walter   *27, 98*

Meinke, Peter   *81*

Modern Times   12

Moore, Todd   *45*

Morgan, Robert   *48, 101*

Morning Glory   16

Most Haunted, The   109

Moving My Grandfather   118

My Mother, If She Had Won Free Dance Lessons   116

Nathan, Leonard   *100*

Nelms, Sheryl L.   *32, 65, 103, 111*

Nemerov, Howard   *16*

Newlyweds 66

No Job   77

No Woman Is Ever Prepared   35

Nolan, James   *12*

Nowlan, Alden   *53*

Nuclear Accident at SL 1, Idaho Falls, 1961, The   8

Nursing Home   117

Old Man & His Calf, The   43

Old Red   43

Oresick, Peter   *68, 107*

Out of the Mines   75

Paley, Grace   *104, 108*

Patriotics   73

Penance, The   100

Piercy, Marge   *79*

Play   20

Poem Ending with an Old Cliché   105

Pulling Peter Back   34

Purple Loosestrife   17

Raising My Hand   1

Recurrence   86

Restoring the Ecology   13

Ridl, Jack   *25*

Rodeo Fool, The   27

Roderick, John M.   *76*

Rogers, Del Marie   *5, 126*

Rosenberg, Liz   *87*

Ruffin, Paul   *47, 120*

Saying Farewell, He Shows Me His Vietnam Poems   102

Schultz, Philip   *56*

Scott, Herbert   *60, 83*

Serchuk, Peter   *41*

Sharkey, Lee   *114*

Shipping Out   92

Simmerman, Jim   *18*

Sister   86

Sklarew, Myra   *15*

Smith, R. T.   *63*

Soniat, Katherine   *96*

Steinbergh, Judith W.   *46, 69*

Strecker, James *50*

Stripped *7*

Suicide's Father, The *33*

Talking Long Distance after One A.M. *57*

Thinking about Bill, Dead of AIDS *36*

To an Estranged Wife *52*

To My Sons on Father's Day *123*

Tom Lonehill (1940–1956) *30*

Torreson, Rodney *84, 93*

Townsend, Ann *17, 20*

Tristem *125*

Twichell, Chase *115*

Two Orders of Love, The *58*

Vietnam War Memorial *101*

View, The *56*

Vinz, Mark *124*

Visiting Paleontologist Feels Her Thigh, The *62*

Vollmer, Judith *8*

Waiting for the Splash *52*

Wallace, Ronald *83, 88*

War *96*

Waters, Mary Ann *97*

Webb, Charles Harper *10*

What Holds Us Back *87*

When Bosses Sank Steel Islands *74*

When Leland Left Elma *55*

White Trash *9*

Why I Quit Dancing Lessons *21*

Why I'm in Favor of a Nuclear Freeze *89*

Why Is It *91*

Williams, Miller *36*

Wilson, Keith *43*

Winter Stars *112*

Wojahn, David *121*

Wood, Susan *108*

Wormser, Baron *33*

wounds #13 *82*

Wrestling to Lose *23*

Young, Gary *52, 75*

Young, Ree *55*

Zimmer, Paul *49, 105*